TOP 10
CHICAGO

ELAINE GLUSAC
ELISA KRONISH
ROBERTA SOTONOFF

D1198526

EYEWITNESS TRAVEL

Left *Nighthawks*, The Art Institute of Chicago Right View from Sears Tower

LONDON, NEW YORK,
MELBOURNE, MUNICH AND DELHI
www.dk.com

Produced by Departure Lounge, London

Reproduced by Colourscan, Singapore
Printed and bound by South China Printing
Co. Ltd., China

First American Edition, 2004
08 09 10 9 8 7 6 5 4 3 2

Published in the United States by
DK Publishing, Inc.,
375 Hudson Street,
New York, New York 10014

Reprinted with revisions 2006, 2008

Copyright 2004, 2008 © Dorling
Kindersley Limited, London
A Penguin Company

A Cataloging in Publication record is available from
the Library of Congress

ISSN 1479-344X
ISBN 978-0-75663-236-6

Within each Top 10 list in this book, no hierarchy
of quality or popularity is implied. All 10 are, in
the editor's opinion, of roughly equal merit.

Floors are referred to throughout in accordance
with British usage; ie the "first floor" is the floor
above ground level.

Contents

Chicago's Top 10

The information in this DK Eyewitness Top 10 Travel Guide is checked regularly.
Every effort has been made to ensure that this book is as up-to-date as possible at the time of going to press. Some details, however, such as telephone numbers, opening hours, prices, gallery hanging arrangements and travel information are liable to change. The publishers cannot accept responsibility for any consequences arising from the use of this book, nor for any material on third party websites, and cannot guarantee that any website address in this book will be a suitable source of travel information. We value the views and suggestions of our readers very highly. Please write to: Publisher, DK Eyewitness Travel Guides, Dorling Kindersley, 80 Strand, London, Great Britain WC2R 0RL.

Cover: Front – **DK Images**: Andrew Leyerle clb; **SuperStock**: Alex Bartel main. Spine – **DK Images**: Andrew Leyerle b. Back – **DK Images**: Andrew Leyerle c, cl, cr.

Left **Frontera Grill** Center **Buddy Guy's Legends** Right **Chicago Blues Festival**

Left **Wave Swinger, Navy Pier** Right **Baha'i Temple, Wilmette**

Key to abbreviations
Adm admission charge payable **Free** no admission charge **DA** disabled access

3

CHICAGO'S
TOP 10

CHICAGO'S TOP 10

🔟 Chicago Highlights

Big-city sophistication combined with small-town hospitality create the perfect blend in this, the Midwest's largest city. Chicago's influential architecture, cuisine for every budget and taste, great shopping, diverse ethnic neighborhoods, and outstanding museums are reason enough for a visit. And the icing on the cake? The city boasts a lakefront and park system that are as beautiful as they are recreational.

1 The Art Institute of Chicago

This grande dame of Chicago's art scene features world-renowned collections. The ever-popular Impressionist section (see pp8–11) includes outstanding exhibits such as Renoir's *Acrobats at the Cirque Fernando*.

2 Sears Tower & its Views

The city's skyscraping superlative is actually made up of nine tube-like sections. The views *(left)* are absolutely awesome: on a clear day, you can see up to 40 miles (64 km) from the 103rd-floor Skydeck (see pp12–13).

3 Field Museum

Delve into cultures and environments from ancient Egypt to modern Africa, via Midwestern wildlife, and the underground life of bugs. The Field also offers a closeup of the world's largest and most complete *Tyrannosaurus rex* skeleton, as well as many other fossils (see pp14–15).

Map labels: Grand Ⓜ, Lake Ⓜ, Washington Ⓜ, WEST WASHINGTON STREET, Washington, Downtown, Monroe Ⓜ, WEST ADAMS STREET, Ⓜ Quincy, Jackson Ⓜ, WEST JACKSON BLVD, LaSalle Ⓜ, Library Ⓜ, WEST CONGRESS PARKWAY, WEST HARRISON STREET, Harrison Ⓜ, SOUTH WACKER DRIVE, SOUTH CLARK STREET

400 — yards — 0 — meters — 400

4 Museum of Science & Industry

An enduring family favorite, this museum is the only building left from the 1893 World's Columbian Exposition. Exhibits emphasizing interactivity cover everything from space exploration to coal-mining, including the Walk-Through Heart and Silver Streak train, which visitors can climb aboard (see pp16–19).

5 Navy Pier

Once dilapidated, this Lake Michigan pier is now a bustling year-round playground for kids and adults alike, complete with a Ferris Wheel and carousel. In warm weather, take a boat tour or join the throngs that stroll along the pier and get some amazing city views (see pp20–21).

6 John G. Shedd Aquarium

Chicago's amazing aquarium is located on the lakefront and is home to thousands of marine animals from big beluga whales to tiny seahorses. Get a fun, fish-eye view at the Oceanarium's underwater viewing galleries (see pp22–3).

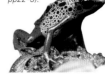

Magnificent Mile

Chicago's premier shopping destination is a four-lane stretch of North Michigan Avenue. It also has historic significance, claiming two of only a few structures to survive the 1871 Great Chicago Fire *(see pp26–7)*.

Lincoln Park Zoo

It might not be the biggest but it's one of the oldest zoos in the country and, after more than 100 years, still free. Kids love the hands-on Pritzker Family Children's Zoo and Endangered Species Carousel *(see pp24–5)*.

The University of Chicago

Opened in 1892, this private university is an important part of the southside Hyde Park neighborhood. Its public attractions include museums and galleries, and a Frank Lloyd Wright home *(see pp28–9)*.

Frank Lloyd Wright's Oak Park

Frank Lloyd Wright, creator of Prairie Style architecture, was based in this Chicago suburb for 20 years. His legacy is an "outdoor museum" of 25 buildings. Take a self-guided or guided tour of his creations and those of other Prairie Style architects *(see pp30–31)*.

The Art Institute of Chicago

Guarded by iconic lions, and up a flight of grand stone steps (a favorite local meeting place) is the Midwest's largest, and one of the USA's best art museums. Housed in a massive Beaux Arts edifice (currently being renovated and expanded), the Institute has some 260,000 works from around the globe, and is famous for its Impressionist and Post-Impressionist works and touring shows.

1 A Sunday on La Grande Jatte–1884

Massive and mesmerizing, this painting took Georges Seurat two years to complete. The scene *(below)* is created from dots of color, based on his study of optical theory, later known as pointillism.

Main museum entrance

● The Garden Restaurant is a lovely lunch stop. Alternatively, cross over to Cosi (116 S. Michigan Ave.) for great sandwiches.

◐ Join a free, hour-long introductory tour. Meet in gallery 100 (1 or 2pm daily)

Don't miss the reconstruction of the 1893 Stock Exchange Trading Room.

In summer, catch live jazz in the Garden Restaurant (4:30–7:30pm Thu)

• 111 S. Michigan Ave.
• Map L6 • El Station: Adams (Green, Orange, Purple, & Yellow lines) Monroe (Blue & Red lines) • 312-443-3600
• www.artic.edu
• Open 10:30am–5pm Mon–Fri (to 8pm Thu); 10am–5pm Sat & Sun.
• Adm: adults $12; students, seniors and children 12 yrs and older $7; under 12 yrs free; free adm 5–8pm Thu •
DA (at both entrances)

Top 10 Paintings

1 *A Sunday on La Grande Jatte–1884*
2 *Acrobats at the Cirque Fernando*
3 *At the Moulin Rouge*
4 *Stacks of Wheat series*
5 *Paris Street; Rainy Day*
6 *Nighthawks*
7 *The Child's Bath*
8 *The Old Guitarist*
9 *The Herring Net*
10 *American Gothic*

2 Acrobats at the Cirque Fernando

Children were often the subjects of Renoir's sunny paintings: this luminous 1879 work shows a circus owner's daughters taking a bow after their act.

3 At the Moulin Rouge

Unlike many of his fellow Impressionists who painted serene, often natural scenes, Toulouse-Lautrec was drawn to the exuberant night- and lowlife of Paris. This dramatic composition (1892) celebrates the famous Moulin Rouge cabaret *(above)*.

4 Stacks of Wheat series

From 1890–91, Monet painted 30 views of the haystacks that stood outside his house at Giverny in France. This museum has six of them, which illustrate the basic Impressionist doctrine of capturing fleeting moments in nature.

5 Paris Street; Rainy Day

Considered to be Gustave Caillebotte's masterpiece, this evocative 1877 view down a Parisian boulevard, with life-sized figures in the foreground, perfectly captures the gray and rainy scene.

Nighthawks
One of the best-known images in 20th-century American Art, this 1942 painting by Realist Edward Hopper has a melancholy quality. It cleverly depicts fluorescent lighting, at the time a recent introduction to US cities.

Michigan Ave. entrance

Key to Floorplan
	Ground Level
	Main Level
	Upper Level

The Child's Bath
The only American to exhibit in Paris with the Impressionists, Mary Cassatt is known for using then-unconventional techniques such as elevated vantage points. She often portrayed women and children as in this, her most famous painting (1892).

The Old Guitarist
A 22-year-old, struggling Picasso painted this tortured 1903 portrait during his Blue Period. This reflected his grief over a friend's suicide and was a precursor to his own style of Cubism.

The Herring Net
Winslow Homer honed his realist skills as an illustrator for magazines and later for the Union during the Civil War. After moving to Maine, he created a series of images, including this one (1885), depicting man's complex relationship with the sea.

American Gothic
Grant Wood borrowed from the detailed style of Flemish Renaissance art to create this much-parodied painting (1930). Though perceived by many as satirical, the painting (left) celebrates rural American values.

Museum Guide
The Art Institute is building an addition to the museum as well as undergoing extensive renovations, all of which will be complete in 2009. The locations of works and the accessibility of specific galleries are subject to change, so if there is a particular work you would like to see, please call ahead first to ensure it is on view.

For more Chicago art galleries and museums See pp38–9

9

Left **Ritual figure, Amerindian Art** Center **Thorne Miniature Rooms** Right **Exhibit, Asian Art**

Collections

European Paintings
Arranged chronologically, and spanning the Middle Age through 1950, this prodigious collection includes a significant array of Renaissance and Baroque art. However, its main draw is a body of nearly 400 Impressionist and Post-Impressionist paintings. Instrumental in its creation was Bertha Honoré Palmer who acquired over 40 Impressionist works (largely ignored in France at the time) for the 1893 World's Columbian Exposition.

American Arts
This impressive holding contains some 5,500 paintings and sculptures dating from the colonial period to 1950. In addition, paintings and works on paper are on loan from the Terra collection and there is a range of decorative arts, including furniture, glass, and ceramics from the 18th century

Vincent Van Gogh, *Self-portrait (1886–7)*, **European Paintings**

Floorplan

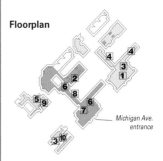

Michigan Ave. entrance

through to the present. The silver collection is especially noteworthy.

Architecture
Given the city's strong architectural heritage and focus, it is not surprising that Chicago's Art Institute boasts an architecture and design department, one of only a few in the US. Sketches and drawings are accessible by appointment, and changing public displays feature models, drawings, and architectural pieces, such as a stained-glass window by Frank Lloyd Wright.

Modern & Contemporary Art
This important collection represents the significant arts movements in Europe and the US from 1950 to the present day, including a strong body of Surrealist works, and notable paintings by Picasso, Matisse, and Kandinsky, as well as showing how American artists, such as Georgia O'Keeffe, interpreted European Modernism. A limited number of artworks will be on view until 2009 while the galleries are being renovated.

For more on Modern Art in Chicago **See pp79, 94–5, 101**

Photography

Spanning the history of the medium, from its origins in 1839 to the present, this eminent collection was started by Georgia O'Keeffe in 1949 with the donation of works by Alfred Stieglitz. Many modern masters, including, Julien Levy, Edward Weston, Paul Strand, and Eugène Atget, are represented.

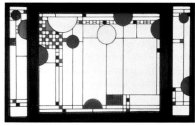

Frank Lloyd Wright art glass, Architecture

Asian Art

This sizeable collection covers 5,000 years and features Chinese ceramics and jades, Japanese screens, and Southeast Asian sculpture. The museum's assemblage of Japanese woodblock prints, such as *Courtesan* (c. 1710) by Kaigetsudo Anchi, is one of the finest outside Japan. Look out, too, for the rare early 14th-century scroll painting, *Legends of the Yuzu Nembutsu*.

African & Amerindian Art

A variety of artifacts, including sculptures, masks, ceramics, furniture, textiles, bead-, gold-, and metal-work, make up this relatively small, but interesting collection. Exhibits from both continents are arranged by region and culture: ceremonial and ritual objects are particularly intriguing.

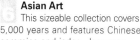

Clematis, Arthur Rubloff paperweight

Arms & Armor

The Harding Collection of Arms and Armor is one of the largest in America. On permanent display are over 200 items related to the art of war including weapons, and complete and partial suits of armor for men – as well as horses. The items displayed originate from Europe, the United States, and the Middle East, and date from the 15th through the 19th centuries.

Arthur Rubloff Paperweight Collection

This fabulous and unusual assemblage numbers in excess of 1,400 paperweights, making it one of the largest of its kind in the world. It showcases colorful and exquisite examples from all periods, designs, and techniques. The paperweights mostly originate from 19th-century France, though some were made in America and the United Kingdom. Displays also reveal the secrets of how paperweights are made.

Thorne Miniature Rooms

Narcissa Ward Thorne, a Chicago art patron, combined her love of miniatures with her interest in interiors and decorative arts to create the 68 rooms in this unique Lilliputian installation. Some of the 1 inch:1 foot scale rooms are replicas of specific historic interiors, while others are period recreations, combining features copied from a variety of sites or based on illustrations and other records of period furniture.

🔟 Sears Tower & its Views

It might have lost the world's tallest building slot to Taipei 101 Tower in Taiwan, thanks to its enormous spire, but Sears Tower (center, left) is still the tallest if measuring the height from ground to roof – a staggering 1,450 ft (442 m). Designed by Chicago firm Skidmore, Owings & Merrill, the tower uses nine exterior frame tubes, avoiding the need for interior supports. On a windy day, workers on higher levels can feel the building sway and hear squeaking noises: you might experience the same thing from the 103rd-floor Skydeck, where on a good day, the 360-degree views – the main draw for visitors – are awesome.

Sears Tower

🍴 The tower has eight restaurants to choose from (open Mon–Fri).

Take an audio Sky Tour to get "inside" information on Chicago at the Skydeck's 16 viewing points.

👁 Check visibility levels at the security desk before you wait in line for the Skydeck.

• 233 S. Wacker Dr. (note: entrance is on Jackson Blvd.)
• 312-875-9696
• Map J4
• www.theskydeck.com
• El Station: Quincy
• Open May–Sep: 10am–10pm daily; Oct–Apr: 10am–8pm daily
• Skydeck adm.: $11.95; children (3–11): $8.50; seniors: $9.95 • DA
• Marina City: 300 N. State St. • Soldier Field: 425 E. McFetridge Dr.
• United Center: 1901 W. Madison St.
• McCormick Place: 2301 S. Lakeshore Dr.

Top 10 Views

1. John Hancock Center
2. Grant Park
3. Soldier Field
4. Navy Pier
5. United Center
6. Marina Towers
7. Merchandise Mart
8. McCormick Place
9. Lake Michigan
10. Chicago River

1 John Hancock Center

The Sears Tower's North Side counterpart is this 100-story skyscraper *(right, center)*. It houses a retail area, offices, and apartments – as well as an open-air observatory on the 94th floor *(see p79)*.

2 Grant Park

Built entirely on land-fill following the Great Chicago Fire *(see p34)* this 200-acre (81-ha) park *(right)* is the city's largest and the site of summer music festivals *(see p62)*.

3 Soldier Field

Home to the Chicago Bears football team *(see p51)* for over 30 years, the 1924-built lakeside stadium *(below)* recently saw the addition of a controversial 63,000-seat structure. Critics have likened it to a padded toilet seat.

Navy Pier
A former naval base turned fun-filled mecca, this is Chicago's leading attraction *(see pp20–21)*.

United Center
This vast indoor sports arena and concert venue *(left)* is also known as 'the house that Michael built,' as it was Michael Jordan's fame that attracted the money to fund it. Outside the center there's a statue of the now-retired, but ever-popular, basketball player.

Marina City
When built in 1964, these distinctive 60-story buildings (nicknamed the corncobs), were both the tallest residential and the tallest concrete structures in the world *(see p36)*.

Merchandise Mart
The largest (in floor area) commercial building in the world, this 1930-built structure covers two blocks and was run by *the* Kennedy family until the late 1990s *(see p79)*.

McCormick Place
The first convention center opened here in 1960 but burned down seven years later. Helmut Jahn built the second in 1971 at twice the size with 40,000 sprinkler heads. Three buildings now make up this complex, and are connected by a shop-lined promenade.

Lake Michigan
This is the third largest of the five Great Lakes. Water temperatures struggle to hit tepid during summer, but many beach-goers swim nevertheless. On a clear day, you can often see across to the shores of Indiana and Michigan.

Chicago River
Chicago's 156-mile (251-km) long river *(above)* tops world records with its 52 opening bridges. An extraordinary engineering feat resulted in the reversal of the river flow in 1900 *(see p34)*. Every St. Patrick's day the main branch is dyed green.

Top 10 Tower Facts

1. It is 110 stories high
2. It weighs 222,500 tonnes
3. The tower took three years to construct
4. Building costs topped $150 million
5. It contains 2,000 miles (3,220 km) of electric cables…
6. … And 25,000 miles (40,233 km) of piping
7. 25,000 people enter and exit each day
8. 1.5 million people visit the Skydeck each year
9. The elevators travel at 1,600 ft (490 m) per minute
10. Six automatic machines wash its 16,100 windows

Field Museum

Founded in 1893 to display items from the World's Columbian Exposition, and renamed in 1905 to honor its first major benefactor, Marshall Field, this vast museum offers fascinating insights into global cultures and environments past and present. Home to all sorts of cultural treasures, fossils, and artifacts, as well as to myriad interactive exhibits, make no bones about it: this natural history museum is one of the best in the country.

Museum façade

🍴 Grab a bite to eat under the watchful gaze of dinosaur Sue at the Corner Bakery on the main level.

🚋 Two free trolley services link the Field, the Shedd (see p22–3) and the Art Institute (see p10–11) with the nearest Metra stations, CTA stations, and Downtown.

Have a museum-related question? Look out for attendants carrying a big "Ask Me" sign.

• 1400 S Lake Shore Dr.
• Map L5
• 312-922-9410
• www.fieldmuseum.org
• Metra station: Roosevelt Road
• Open 9am–5pm daily
• Adm.: adults $12, children (4–11), seniors, and students with ID $7
• DA

Top 10 Exhibits

1. Sue
2. Pacific Spirits
3. Underground Adventure
4. Lions of Tsavo
5. Inside Ancient Egypt
6. Grainger Hall of Gems
7. Hall of Jades
8. Africa
9. Pawnee Earth Lodge
10. Nature Walk

Pacific Spirits
A real celebration of vibrant Pacific islander culture: visitors can see dramatic masks (above), listen to recorded sounds from the swamps of New Guinea, and bang on an impressive 9-ft (3-m) drum.

Underground Adventure
Enter this larger-than-life "subterranean" ecosystem to get a bug's-eye view of life. Wander through a jungle of roots (right), and listen to the chatter of a busy ant colony. Extra admission charged.

Sue

A Tyrannosaurus rex, 13-ft (4-m) high by 42-ft (12.8-m) long – the largest, most complete, and best preserved ever found. Her real 600-lb (272-kg) skull, too heavy for the skeleton, is on view nearby.

Lions of Tsavo
In 1898, these two partners in crime killed and ate 140 men constructing a bridge in Kenya, before they in turn were hunted and killed. The skins were first used as rugs, before being mounted as you see today.

5 Inside Ancient Egypt

This part-original, part-replica Egyptian ruin leads you up and down stairs, into Egyptian bedrooms and tombs, and even through a marketplace. Discover how Cleopatra lived and how mummies were wrapped.

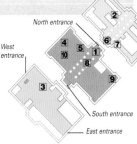

North entrance

West entrance

South entrance

East entrance

Key to Floorplan

▦	Ground Level
▦	Main Level
▦	Upper Level

6 Grainger Hall of Gems

Fiber-optic lighting illuminates over 500 glittering gems, precious stones, and minerals. Even though it's a replica, the star of the show is the breath-taking Hope Diamond.

7 Hall of Jades

This impressive collection of over 500 jade artifacts includes items from Neolithic burial sites, the Chinese Dynasties and the early 20th century. Tools used to create them are also on display.

Museum Guide

The main entrance is located on the museum's north side, though visitors typically enter on the south, where buses, trolleys, and cabs drop off. A third (ground level) west entrance is suitable for wheelchair access. If you visit on a weekday, it's worth asking staff about the museum's Free Highlights Tours, which take place twice daily. And don't forget to look for information on the day's special events, tours, and activities, posted throughout the building.

8 Africa

Browse the wares of a Saharan market, experience life on a slave ship, and see a pair of fighting elephants *(left)*: this exhibit offers an amazing journey through ancient and modern Africa.

9 Pawnee Earth Lodge

This replica Pawnee dwelling is an interactive exhibit that showcases the traditions of the 19th-century Pawnee Indians.

10 Nature Walk

Stroll through wetland, woodland, and other habitat dioramas complete with stuffed wildlife striking perfect poses. A deer management computer game lets you play God with the fate of the animals.

Chicago's Top 10

Museum of Science & Industry

The cultural star of the city's Far South, this museum was the first in North America to introduce interactive exhibits, with a record of innovative, hands-on displays dating back to the 1930s. More than one million visitors flock annually to this vast neoclassical building, which houses more than 800 exhibits and is a Chicago must-see, especially for families. Make sure you arrive rested, since it takes a whole day to hit just the top attractions.

Great Hall entrance

🍴 The Brain Food Court serves above-average fare including wood-fired pizzas, and made-to-order salads and sandwiches.

🎫 Advance tickets reserved on the Internet or telephone cost an extra $2 each but are worth it on busy weekends.

Additional Omnimax tickets can be bought for $6 (adults) and $5 (children 3–11) at all museum entrances.

• 57th Street & Lake Shore Drive
• Map F6
• 1-773-684-1414
• www.msichicago.org
• Metra station: 55th/56th/57th
• Open 9:30am–4pm Mon–Sat, 11am–4pm Sun
• Adm.: adults $11, children (3–11) $7; including one Omnimax show: adults $17, children $12 • DA

Top 10 Features

1. Apollo 8 Command Module
2. The Great Train Story
3. Walk-Through Heart
4. The Coal Mine
5. Colleen Moore's Fairy Castle
6. All Aboard the Silver Streak
7. Yesterday's Main Street
8. Omnimax Theater
9. Toy Maker 3000
10. U-505 Submarine

1 Apollo 8 Command Module

This, the first manned spacecraft to orbit the moon, offers a genuine peek into the 1960s space race. The historic photos, space suits, and training module on display all help set the scene.

3 Walk-Through Heart

A museum favorite since the 1940s, this 20-ft (6-m) tall model of the human heart would fit inside the chest of a 28-story person. Enter its chambers to see the marvel of human engineering.

2 The Great Train Story

Thirty-four miniature trains (below) race past sky-scrapers, through prairies, and over the Rockies to the Pacific Docks on 1,425 ft (437 m) of track that replicates the 2,200-mile (3540 km) train trip from Chicago to Seattle.

4 The Coal Mine

Venture down a simulated 600 ft (184 m) in an authentic shaft elevator to discover how coal was extracted in the 1930s compared to today. The mini train ride enhances the underground illusion.

Colleen Moore's 5 Fairy Castle

Star of the silent screen, Colleen Moore commissioned the design of this lavish 9-sq-ft (0.8 sq-m) castle *(left)* and lovingly filled it with over 2,000 one-twelfth-scaled objects, including the world's smallest Bible.

Space Center entrance

Great Hall entrance

Key to Floorplan

	Ground Level
	Main Level
	Upper Level

All Aboard the 6 Silver Streak

Both Art Deco design afficionados and rail buffs alike are drawn to this streamlined, vintage Zephyr train with its ground-breaking diesel-electric engine. Onboard visits are by tour only.

Yesterday's 7 Main Street

A cobblestone, shop-lined street gives a taste of 1910 Chicago, with a cinema screening free silent movies and a tradi-tional ice-cream parlor serving sweet treats at present-day prices.

Omnimax Theater 8

Films shown in this five-story theater make the viewers feel like they are right in the thick of the on-screen adventures. Films on a rotating pro-gram are screened about every 50 minutes.

ToyMaker 3000 9

Twelve robotic arms work the assembly line to produce toy top after colorful top in this display of computer integrated manufacturing tech-nology. You can race a robot to see who can trace letters faster, and souvenir tops come gratis.

U-505 Submarine 10

Take a tour around this 1941 German U-boat: captured during World War II, it looks much as it did then, complete with an Enigma codebreaking machine.

Museum Guide

The museum has two main entrances – the Great Hall (ground level) and the Henry Crown Space Center entrance (for the Omnimax Theater). Head first to tour-only displays – the Silver Streak, U-505, and the Coal Mine – as later in the day waits for these can be more than an hour. If purchasing Omnimax tickets choose a later time, when you'll truly appreciate sitting down. Strollers can be rented for $2 in the Great Hall.

Left **Communications Zone** Right **Boeing 727, Transportation Zone**

Exhibits

Transportation Zone
A full-size Boeing 727 and a British World War II fighter plane dangle dramatically above a steam locomotive and the world's fastest land vehicle, while visitors explore the forces of flight via computer games and videos.

U-505
Artifacts, archival footage, and interactive challenges bring to life this restored U-505 German submarine. Optional on-board tours of the boat are available.

Genetics: Decoding Life
Explore the complex and controversial world of genetics and genetic engineering and learn how cloning is possible, while viewing real cloned mice.

The Farm
Learn about life on today's farms and the modern technologies that get food from the field to your table. Children can ride in a real combine and take part in a cow-milking challenge.

Boiler Clock

Networld
The binary world of cyberspace comes alive here via educational yet fun hands-on displays.

AIDS: The War Within
Replicas of enlarged human cells vividly illustrate the in-depth workings of the HIV virus in this highly educational exhibit.

Museum Floorplan

Main Level

Ground Level

Upper Level

Entrance

Ships Through the Ages
Here, model ships chart marine transportation from Egyptian sailboats through to modern ocean liners. Highlights include scale versions of Christopher Columbus' three ships.

Petroleum Planet
The journey from pipeline to polymers is told from an oil molecule's perspective, ending in a huge display of by-products, from running shoes to chewing gum.

Communications Zone
The Whispering Gallery illustrates how sound-waves make even the faintest whisper audible at the other end of a room, while the World Live Theater lets visitors witness TV broadcasts being beamed in from around the world.

Enterprise
Interactive scenarios allow visitors to climb into the shoes of a fictional CEO to lead a toy manufacturing company through important business decisions.

Top 10 Features of the 1893 Exposition

The Museum's Origins

Built as the Palace of Fine Arts in 1893, the Museum of Science and Industry is now the only building left from Daniel Burnham's vast "White City." This was constructed for the World's Columbian Exposition, which marked the 400th anniversary (albeit one year late) of Christopher Columbus' arrival in the New World. Burnham, the Director of Works for the fair (see p37), commissioned architects like Charles Atwood to create structures that would showcase the best in design, culture, and technology. The Field Museum (see pp14–15) inhabited the building until the 1920s when it moved to its present-day Museum Campus home. Sears Roebuck retail chief Julius Rosenwald then decided that a fortified palace, stripped to its steel frame and rebuilt in limestone, would be the perfect home for a new museum devoted to "industrial enlightenment" and US technological achievements. Appropriately, the Museum debuted in 1933 when Chicago hosted its next World's Fair, the Century of Progress Exposition.

A stone figure on the Museum

The Restoration

Although built to withstand fire, due to the value of its contents, the Palace of Fine Arts was originally intended as a post-Fair tear-down, so it needed massive reconstruction when Rosenwald decided to restore it to its former glory in the 1920s. The financial support of many local business men and the city of Chicago helped him to fulfill this dream.

The Museum as it stands today

🔟 Navy Pier

As recently as 1995 Chicago's Navy Pier was a drab slab of concrete projecting into Lake Michigan, formerly used as a military and freight terminal. But a huge effort to funnel locals and tourists onto the Pier has seen the installation of a variety of attractions on the waterfront – for kids as well as adults – that draw over eight million people annually, making this Chicago's most visited attraction. An added bonus of spending time at the Pier: the breathtaking city views.

Navy Pier

📍 Skip the chain eateries in favor of ribs and live jazz at Joe's Be-Bop Café.

In summer the beer garden at the far end of the Pier offers stellar city views as well as free bands.

🏃 Join a 90-minute lake tour *(see p111)* on a four-masted schooner, or take a ride on a Seadog speedboat.

Save money and time spent in line with a combination ticket for the Musical Carousel, Ferris Wheel, and Wave Swinger.

• 600 E. Grand Avenue
• Map M3
• 1-800-595-7437
• www.navypier.com
• CTA Bus: 29; 65; 56; 66; 120; 121 • Open summer: 10am–10pm daily (to midnight Fri & Sat); Sep & Oct: 10am–9pm Mon–Sat (to 11pm Fri & Sat), 10am–7pm Sun; winter: 10am–8pm Mon–Sat (to 10pm Fri & Sat), 10am–7pm Sun
• Free entrance but many attractions charge • DA

Top 10 Exhibits

1 Wave Swinger
2 Chicago Children's Museum
3 Skyline Stage
4 Smith Museum of Stained-Glass Windows
5 Musical Carousel
6 Ferris Wheel
7 Chicago Shakespeare Theater
8 IMAX® Theatre
9 Amazing Chicago's Funhouse Maze
10 Miniature Golf Course

Chicago Children's Museum
Kids love this hands-on museum that educates through play. Under-twos get dedicated spaces, including a water room, with clothing protection provided *(see p56)*.

Wave Swinger
Each of the 48 chain-suspended chairs on this colorful, old-fashioned thrill ride lifts riders 14 ft (5 m) in the air, and spins them until the skyline blurs *(below)*.

Pepsi Skyline Stage
During the summer this unique 1500-seat theater, with its state-of-the-art acoustics, hosts ticketed pop, rock, folk, and jazz concerts against a stunning backdrop. Children's theater, dance performances, and other live events are also staged in this intimate setting.

Smith Museum of Stained-Glass Windows
The first museum of its kind in the USA, the Smith displays 150 artworks made of colored glass *(above)* along 800 ft (240 m) of the Pier's interior corridors. Highlights include 13 pieces from Louis Comfort Tiffany's workshop.

Plan of Navy Pier

Musical Carousel

A quaint merry-go-round of 36 hand-painted horses and chariots located next to the Ferris Wheel replicates a similar ride installed on the Pier in the 1920s.

Ferris Wheel

It's hard to miss the Pier's 15-story Ferris Wheel. The slowly and continually revolving ride seats six passengers in each of its 40 enclosed cars. Daytime rides offer fine lake views, while evening rides show off the magical city lights.

Chicago Shake-speare Theater

This highly renowned theater aims to make the Bard accessible to the pleasure-seeking masses visiting Navy Pier. As well as Shakespearean standards, productions also include the "Short Shakespeare" series for younger audiences.

IMAX® Theatre

The six-story, 80-ft- (24-m) wide flatscreen movie theater offers celluloid fare ranging from scientific documentaries to Disney features. Sound and vision headsets aid 3D movie enjoyment.

Amazing Chicago's Funhouse Maze

This mirror-filled, Chicago-themed walking maze leads you on a disorienting, 15-minute trip. Expect spinning lights, startling sound effects, and new perspectives on city sights.

Miniature Golf Course

Putt your way around Pier Park via the 18 holes of this mini-golf course, situated at the base of the Pier's Ferris Wheel. Each hole has a Chicago theme and the course is suitable for all ages.

Orientation

Take public transit, a taxi, or walk to Navy Pier. If driving, there are over 1600 parking spaces right on the Pier. Once there, be sure to stop off at the Guest Services desk, just inside the main entrance, to pick up a schedule for details of the day's events, including performance times and locations for the resident comedy troupe, brass band, and a capella singing group.

John G. Shedd Aquarium

The eponymous John G. Shedd, president of Marshall Field's department store (see p74), donated this Beaux Arts aquarium to Chicago in 1929. One of the city's top attractions ever since, it houses some 25,500 marine animals representing 2,100 different species that include amphibians, fish, and aquatic mammals. The latter romp in the saltwater of the 1991-built glass-walled Oceanarium, which places an infinity pool in front of Lake Michigan to transporting effect.

The Oceanarium

🍴 Choose one of three dining options at the Shedd: the sit-down Soundings serves upscale fare with stellar lake views; the Bubble Net Food Court offers pizzas, sandwiches, and burgers; or you can brown bag it at one of the picnic tables.

🎯 Don't miss the Shedd's underwater viewing galleries.

Check out Jazzin' at the Shedd on Thursdays (5–10pm, adm $10) from June through August.

• 1200 S. Lake Shore Dr.
• Map M6
• 312-939-2438 •
www.sheddaquarium.org
• El station: Roosevelt (Green, Orange, & Red lines) • Open summer (Memorial Day to Labor Day): 9am–6pm daily, (to 10pm Thu Jun–Aug); winter: 9am–5pm Mon–Fri, 9am–6pm Sat & Sun
• Adm.: $23; children (3–11) & seniors $16. 4-D All-Access Pass: $27.50; children and seniors $20.50 • DA

Top 10 Exhibits

1. Caribbean Coral Reef
2. Oceanarium
3. Wild Reef
4. Habitat Chats
5. Waters of the World
6. Special Exhibit Gallery
7. Amazon Rising
8. Animal Enounters
9. 4-D Special FX Theater
10. Oceanarium Shows

Caribbean Coral Reef
This vibrant tropical tank contains glinting tarpon, bonnethead sharks, fluttering rays, and many other fish. A scuba diver hand-feeds them six times daily *(right)*, narrating his task via an underwater microphone.

Wild Reef
Gain a daring diver's perspective of whitetip reef, blacktip reef, sandbar, and zebra sharks. The Sawfish and fearsome Lionfish *(left)* happily hold their own amid the predator school.

Oceanarium
Underwater galleries afford incredible views of the likes of dolphins and beluga whales swimming through the Oceanarium's vast pools. It is bordered by rocky outcrops and towering pines in an amazing re-creation of the Pacific Northwest coast.

Habitat Chats
Oceanarium staffers hold daily discussions about the beluga whales, sea otters, and gentoo and rockhopper penguins in their charge. Twice daily there are also chats covering a changing roster of fish from the aquarium.

5 Waters of the World

Themed tanks hold over 90 recreated aquatic habitats, including Ocean Coasts, Tropical Waters, and Africa, Asia, and Australia. An Australian lungfish, known as "Grandad", has been a resident since 1933.

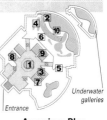

Aquarium Plan

6 Special Exhibit Gallery

This 3,600 sq ft (334 sq m) special exhibit gallery is located on the mezzanine level of the Oceanarium and features changing exhibits focused on aquatic animals.

7 Amazon Rising

Demonstrating the huge seasonal tides of the world's longest river, this exhibit presents a year in the life of the Amazon flood plain. Look out for the ferocious red-bellied piranha (above).

8 Animal Encounters

Get up close and personal with Chilean rose tarantulas, African bullfrogs, and red-tailed boas in handler-controlled encounters, twice daily.

9 4-D Special FX Theater

The whole family will enjoy this hi-tech theater experience. The "special FX seats" bombard the spectator with bubbles, wind, smells, sounds, and all manner of surprises.

10 Oceanarium Shows

Four or five times a day trainers put the belugas (left) and dolphins through their paces. Children are chosen from the audience to reward the animals' intrepid feats (such as tail-walking, and vocalizing) with tasty treats.

Aquarium Guide

Consult the day's event schedule – which is printed on the map you're given – to get the most out of your visit. Try to arrive 10–15 minutes early for an Oceanarium Show to get the best seats, and remember that the 20–30 minute Habitat Chats often follow the shows. There are special events for the little ones on Tuesdays – call the Aquarium for more information.

Chicago's Top 10

🔟 Lincoln Park Zoo

Chicago's second most popular attraction after Navy Pier, this menagerie is not only one of the oldest zoos in the country but also one of the last not to charge admission. Established in 1868 with just a pair of swans, its age helps to account for how well integrated it is with the surrounding North Side community. While small compared to lots of top US zoos, it is a leading light for ape research, and its park setting, duck ponds, historic café, and landmark red barn endear it to all who visit.

Entrance, Lincoln Park Zoo

🍴 Check out the Mexican fare year round at the Park Place Café. In summer, grab a pizza at the historic Café Brauer, which also has a beer garden – rare in the usually alcohol-free Chicago parks.

❓ Have any animal-related questions? If so, ask staffers at the "Discovery Carts" located all around the zoo.

- 2200 N. Cannon Drive
- Map F3
- 312-742-2000
- www.lpzoo.org
- CTA bus 151; 156
- Grounds open: 9am–6pm daily.
- Buildings open summer & fall: 10am–5pm daily (summer: to 6:30pm Sat, Sun & hols); winter: 10am–4:30pm daily • Adm: free but $2 charge for Endangered Species Carousel
- Parking: $12 • DA

Top 10 Exhibits

1. Polar Bear Pool
2. Small Mammal-Reptile House
3. Regenstein African Journey
4. Endangered Species Carousel
5. Regenstein Center for African Apes
6. Bird House
7. Pritzker Family Children's Zoo
8. Lion House
9. Sea Lion Pool
10. Farm-in-the-Zoo

1 Polar Bear Pool

The highlight of this recently remodeled pool is the underwater viewing window through which zoo-goers can spy the beautiful sibling bears pawing their way through the water *(below)*.

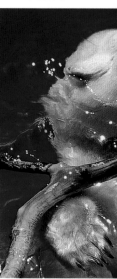

2 Small Mammal-Reptile House

Replicating the warm climes of South America, Asia, Africa, and Australia, this exhibit introduces the exotic worlds of animals such as snakes *(below)*.

3 Regenstein African Journey

Elephants, rhinos, hippos, giraffes, and wild dogs are among the many animals to roam this expansive exhibit. Begin your walking adventure and experience total immersion in the sights and sounds of the varied African landscape around you.

4 Endangered Species Carousel

Ride a wooden tiger or a bamboo-munching panda on this tent-topped merry-go-round devoted to almost 50 endangered species, many of which are represented in the zoo itself. Admission is charged for this attraction.

For information on the neighboring Lincoln Park Conservatory See p86

5 Regenstein Center for African Apes

Simulating the natural habitat of chimps and gorillas, this exhibit offers huge indoor, tri-level spaces rigged with lifelike trees and vines, as well as an outdoor yard for use in summer.

Lincoln Park Zoo Plan

6 Bird House

Here, a series of habitats showcase their native bird species. And a walk-through tropical aviary allows you to have a close encounter with 20 exotic and endangered species, such as the African fairy bluebird.

7 Pritzker Family Children's Zoo

Children of all ages can feel "at home in the woods" while visiting animals native to North America, including Black Bears and Spotted Turtles.

8 Lion House

This 1912 structure stands out not only for its grand architecture but also the grand inhabitants. Many kinds of big cats, including Siberian Tigers, prowl – and roar – both inside the hall and in outdoor enclosures.

10 Farm-in-the-Zoo Presented by John Deere

Keeping city kids in touch with their Midwestern roots, this exhibit offers a daily roster of activities such as goat-milking, cow-feeding, and butter-churning, and the chance to see chicks being born.

9 Sea Lion Pool

Despite the name, harbor and gray seals inhabit this pool. Watch them play at the pool's edge or through an under-ground viewing window. Try to catch the 2pm feeding session (above).

Visitor Guide

Stop by the Gateway Pavilion, just inside the east gate, when you arrive at the zoo. There, you can pick up a free visitor guide to find out about feeding times and special events. Staff are on hand here to provide extra information about any new animal arrivals or exhibits. Parking facil-ities, lockers, strollers, and wheelchairs are also available there.

TOP 10 Magnificent Mile

This glitzy strip of stores and striking buildings runs for, you guessed it, about a mile (1.6 km), along North Michigan Avenue. A sharp developer came up with the "magnificent" moniker in 1947, and it has stuck ever since. Often known as the Mag Mile, it is home to big-guns department stores like Neiman Marcus, as well as high-end boutiques such as Tiffany & Co, and popular chain stores (Gap et al). The strip is at its best around Christmas when twinkling trimmings provide welcome relief from the often gray days.

North Michigan Ave. Bridge

◯ Choose from a wide range of high-end, global, fast food at Foodlife food court in Water Tower Place.

◐ The Pumping Station has a visitor center and a Hot Tix booth (open 10am–6pm Tue–Sat, 11am–4pm Sun) for reduced same-day theater tickets *(see p80).*

• Map L2–3
• Visitor Information 312-642-3570
• www.themagnificent mile.com
• El Station: Grand/State; Chicago/State
• Water Tower Place Mall: 835 N. Michigan Ave., 312-440-3166, open 10am–8pm Mon–Thu, 10am–10pm Fri, 8am– 10pm Sat, 12–6pm Sun
• Garrett Popcorn Shop: 670 N. Michigan Ave., 312-944-2630, hours vary

Top 10 Features

1. The Drake Hotel
2. John Hancock Center
3. Water Tower Place
4. Historic Water Tower & Pumping Station
5. American Girl Place
6. Hershey's Chicago
7. Garrett Popcorn Shop
8. Hotel Intercontinental
9. Tibune Tower
10. Wrigley Building

① The Drake Hotel
This elegant hotel became an instant glamor hot spot when it opened on New Year's Eve in 1920. Marilyn Monroe was among the many stars who have graced it with their presence. High tea in the lobby café is a real treat *(see p115).*

② John Hancock Center
When this sleek 100-story building was built in 1970, it was the world's tallest. Exhilarating views of Chicago and beyond are afforded by the 94th-floor observatory and adjoining open-air area, the Skywalk *(see pp76–7).*

③ Water Tower Place
Housing one of the city's busiest shopping malls, this multi-use complex is one of the world's tallest reinforced concrete buildings. Its 100-plus shops include branches of Macy's and Lord & Taylor department stores.

④ Historic Water Tower & Pumping Station
Dwarfed by the surrounding skyscrapers, these structures are among the few that survived the Great Fire of 1871. The water tower *(left)* now contains an art gallery, while the pumping station still functions and also houses a visitor center *(see p80).*

5 American Girl Place

Eager girls and their loving moms swarm to this palace of little-girliness *(see p82)*, which all kind of merchandise from the popular American Girl doll range. Try the store café *(see p57)* or attend the surprisingly acclaimed musical performances.

Magnificent Mile Map

6 Hershey's Chicago

North America's largest chocolate manufacturer offers a themed retail experience in its Chicago store. Old favorites such as *Hershey's Reese's* and *Kit Kat* are on sale alongside the latest new products *(see p81)*.

7 Garrett Popcorn Shop

A Chicago fixture since 1949, this beloved popcorn shop seduces mind-boggling numbers of people, who snake through its huge lines to get their bag of caramel, cheese, buttered or plain.

8 Hotel Inter-Continental

Built in 1929 as a luxury club for the all-male Shrine association, this amazing hotel *(see p115)* reveals a range of flamboyant architectural styles in its public spaces. Take a self-guided tour to see the highlights, including the stunning swimming pool *(above)*.

9 Tribune Tower

The result of a design competition organized by the *Chicago Tribune* newspaper, this Gothic tower *(above, right)* is either adored or abhorred by locals. Either way, it's a dramatic Mag Mile landmark *(see p80)*.

10 Wrigley Building

The two towers of the former Wrigley headquarters add to Michigan Avenue's exciting skyline *(above left)*. At night, colored lights illuminate them, as they have done since the building opened in 1921 *(see p61)*.

Bridge to Success

The North Michigan Avenue bascule bridge, built in 1920, was the first of its kind in the world. Instrumental in Chicago's northward expansion, it provides a fitting gateway to the city's main retail artery – the Mag Mile. The southwest tower houses the McCormick Tribune Bridgehouse and River Museum, which details the history of Chicago River and displays the interworkings of this landmark drawbridge.

⑩ The University of Chicago

With Chicago's expansion in the late 19th century, a major university was the perfect addition to an array of new cultural institutions. Funded by oil magnate John D. Rockefeller, (who deemed it his best ever investment) the forward-thinking institution opened in 1892. Today, the university is one of the USA's most respected, boasting 78 Nobel prize winners as students, faculty, or researchers, as well as several on-campus attractions that are destinations in their own right.

Cobb Gate

🍴 Go for a deep-dish pizza at a Chicago favorite, Girodano's (5311 S. Blackstone Ave.).

🎵 Rockefeller memorial chapel's carillon is played Oct–Jun 6pm Mon–Fri, noon Sun, Jun–Sep, every Sun.

- 5801 S. Ellis Ave.
- 1-773-702-1234
- www.uchicago.edu
- Map E6
- Metra Station: 55th/56th/57th Sts.; 59th St.
- Bond Chapel: open 8am–4:45pm daily, Free,
- Smart Museum of Art: open 10am–4pm Tue–Fri (to 8pm Thu); 11am–5pm Sat & Sun, Jun–Sep, Free
- Cobb Hall: Renaissance society open 10am–5pm Tue–Fri, noon–5pm Sat & Sun, Free
- Rockefeller Memorial Chapel: open 8am–4pm daily (except during services), Free
- Regenstein Library: special collections exhibits open to the public 8:30am–4:45pm Mon–Fri, Sat 9am–12.45pm term-time, Free

Top 10 Features

1. Oriental Institute
2. Bond Chapel
3. Smart Museum of Art
4. Main Quadrangle
5. Robie House
6. Cobb Gate
7. *Nuclear Energy*
8. Rockefeller Memorial Chapel
9. Cobb Hall
10. Regenstein Library

① Oriental Institute
The institute's amazing museum *(see p99)* has five galleries that showcase the history, art, and archaeology of the ancient Near East. Don't miss the Egyptian Gallery's towering 17-ft (5.2-m) statue of King Tutankhamun *(right)*.

② Bond Chapel
Built in 1926, this small, ivy-covered chapel features exterior stone carvings of angels, imps, and Adam and Eve. Inside, stained-glass windows illustrate scenes from the New Testament *(below)*.

③ Smart Museum of Art
Magazine moguls David and Alfred Smart founded this museum in 1974. It might be small, but its contents (ranging from ancient ceramics to 20th-century sculpture) pack an impressive punch.

④ Main Quadrangle
Rejecting post-Civil War modernity, Henry Ives Cobb's 1891 campus plan mimics England's Gothic Oxford University, with this main unifying quad surrounded by smaller ones.

Unless otherwise stated, all attractions have Disabled Access.

Robie House
Frank Lloyd Wright described his striking low-rise, Prairie-style masterpiece as "the cornerstone of modern architecture." The not-so-humble architect built it in 1909 for bicycle manufacturer Frederick C. Robie (see p100).

Cobb Gate
This ornate northern entrance to the Main Quad is adorned with gargoyles. University lore says they represent students' four years of college life: from struggling freshman at the base to graduation at the apex.

Nuclear Energy
This 12-ft (3.65-m) bulbous bronze sculpture by Henry Moore marks the general area where Enrico Fermi and his team of scientists achieved the first controlled self-sustaining nuclear chain reaction in 1942.

Rockefeller Memorial Chapel
The tallest building on campus is this mini-cathedral named for university patron John D. Rockefeller. It boasts magnficent stained glass, a 72-bell carillon (the world's second largest), and a 10,000-pipe organ.

Cobb Hall
Confusingly, the oldest building on campus is not named for its architect, Henry Cobb, but for an unrelated donor, Silas Cobb. Built in 1882, the beautiful Gothic structure houses classrooms, offices, and the Renaissance Society, a contemporary art gallery.

Robie House **5**

EAST 58TH STREET

1 Oriental Institute

8 Rockefeller Memorial Chapel

100 ⌐ yards ¬0⌐meters ⌐100

Top 10 Alumni

1. Milton Friedman (1912–2006), economist
2. James D. Watson, (1928–), scientist
3. Philip Glass (1937–), composer/musician
4. Edwin Hubble (1889–1953), astronomer
5. Susan Sontag (1933–2005), critic/author
6. Eliot Ness (1903–57), author/law enforcer
7. John Ashcroft (1942–), US Attorney General
8. Philip Roth (1933–), author
9. Carl Sagan (1934–96), astronomer/author
10. Studs Terkel (1912–), oral historian

Regenstein Library
The 1970-built limestone "Reg," (above) honors Chicago industrialist Joseph Regenstein. Exceptional jazz archives, map collections, and children's books feature among its seven million plus volumes.

Frank Lloyd Wright's Oak Park

This quiet suburb, seven miles (11 km) west of downtown Chicago, contains the world's largest collection of Frank Lloyd Wright-designed buildings. It was here that Wright developed his Prairie style, (inspired by the flat lines of the Midwestern plains), influencing other architects such as George Maher. His work was first considered radical, even ugly, compared to the typical styles of the day. Walking through Oak Park's quaint, tree-lined streets, it's evident that Wright's unique architecture does stand out from the norm – but in all the right ways.

Detail of house in Oak Park designed by Wright

○ Dine Italian at family-run La Bella Pasteria (1103 South Blvd., 1-708-524-0044)

○ The Visitors' Center sells maps, books, and tickets for area tours (158 N. Forest Ave., 1-708-848-1500)

- Map A5
- El Station: Oak Park
- Frank Lloyd Wright Home & Studio, 951 Chicago Avenue, 1-708-848-1976, www.wright plus.org, open daily, tour times vary, no DA
- Unity Temple, 875 West Lake Street
- Pleasant Home, 217 South Home Avenue
- Arthur Heurtley House, 318 Forest Avenue
- The Bootleg Houses, 1019/1027/1031 Chicago Avenue
- Charles Matthews House, 432 North Kenilworth Avenue
- Edwin Cheney House, 520 North East Avenue
- Beachy House, 238 Forest Avenue
- Nathan Moore House, 333 Forest Avenue
- Harry Adams House, 710 Augusta Boulevard

Top 10 Buildings

1. Unity Temple
2. Frank Lloyd Wright Home & Studio
3. Pleasant Home
4. Arthur Heurtley House
5. Beachy House
6. Charles Matthews House
7. Edwin Cheney House
8. The Bootleg Houses
9. Nathan Moore House
10. Harry Adams House

1 Unity Temple

This compact church (1908) wonderfully demonstrates Wright's use of poured concrete for both structural and decorative purposes *(right)*.

2 Frank Lloyd Wright Home & Studio

Built when Wright moved to Oak Park (1889), this is where he designed over 150 structures *(above)*. The children's playroom is luminous with signature art-glass windows.

3 Pleasant Home

This 30-room Prairie-style 1897 home built by George Maher, was Oak Park's first to have electricity. It holds a small history museum, including exhibits relating to Tarzan creator and former local resident, Edgar Rice Burroughs.

4 Arthur Heurtley House

Wright's beautiful 1902 house *(above)* is absolute Prairie, with its low, wide chimney, and band of art-glass windows that makes the over-hanging roof appear to float.

For detailed information on opening hours call the Visitors' Center. Most buildings open to the public are visited by tour only.

5 Beachy House

An impressive 1906 home that contradicts many of Wright's trademarks. Instead of just stucco and wood or brick and concrete, he used them all: it also has a seven-gabled, rather than a hipped, roof.

Oak Park Street Map

6 Charles Matthews House

Architects Thomas Eddy Tallmadge and Vernon S. Watson designed this elegant 1909 Prairie-style residence for a wealthy druggist. Among the interior details are Prairie-inspired light fixtures and folding art-glass doors.

7 Edwin Cheney House

Now a B&B, this home sparked a tragic love affair between Wright and Mrs. Cheney, leading him to abandon his family and practice. Mamah Cheney and her children were murdered at Wright's Wisconsin home by an insane servant in 1914.

8 The Bootleg Houses

Wright lost his job over these three private commissions, built while he was actually employed by Louis Sullivan (see p37). Though Queen Anne-like in style, they hint at the design elements that were to be his hallmarks.

9 Nathan Moore House

Out of financial desperation, Wright built this charming Tudor-style home (above) for his neighbor. After a fire destroyed the top floors in 1922, Wright's modifications echoed his West Coast concrete block houses.

10 Harry Adams House

This striking 1913 home marks the last of Wright's Oak Park houses and features several of the elements that made him famous, such as exquisite stained glass, and a low overhanging roof.

Frank Lloyd Wright

After moving to Oak Park in 1889, Wright (1867–1959) appeared to lead the perfect suburban life. But in the early 20th century he created scandals by galavanting with married women, and wearing flamboyant clothes and long hair. During the Depression, however, he transformed into a respected social visionary, and later redefined himself as a quick-witted sage. Ultimately, though, he became a master of self-promotion, establishing himself as the first celebrity architect.

Literary buffs take note: Ernest Hemingway's Oak Park birthplace is open to the public (339 N.Oak Park Ave., 1-708-848-2222)

31

Chicago's Top 10

Great Chicago Fire of 1871

TOP 10 Moments in Chicago History

1871: Great Chicago Fire
Over 250 people died and 17,000 buildings were destroyed in this fire, allegedly started by a cow kicking over a lantern. Just a few buildings survived, including the Historic Water Tower and Pumping Station *(see p80)*.

2 1885: First Skyscraper
Though just a measly – by today's standards – nine stories, the Home Insurance Building (now demolished) was the tallest of its time. William LeBarron Jenney achieved this architectural feat by designing the first weight-bearing steel frame. From then on, the only way was up.

3 1886: Haymarket Riot
Wealthy industrialists funded amazing Chicago arts institutions, but their workers toiled long hours in abominable conditions. In May 1886, a labor protest ended in an explosion at Haymarket Square that killed eight policemen and two bystanders. Eight anarchists were convicted of murder, though three were later pardoned for lack of evidence.

4 1892: First Elevated Train
The first train traveled just 3.6 miles (5.8 km) along tracks built above city-owned alleys, (avoiding the need to negotiate with private property owners). By 1893, the line was extended to Jackson Park *(see p62)* to transport visitors to the World's Columbian Exposition *(see p19)*.

5 1900: Reversal of the Chicago River
With sewage flowing downriver to Lake Michigan, the source of the city's drinking water, thousands of Chicagoans were dying from the contamination. To solve the problem, engineers created a canal that forced the river to flow away from the lake: an extraordinary feat of modern engineering.

Al Capone

6 1919: Chicago Black Sox Scandal
The Chicago White Sox was a winning baseball team but poorly paid, so players sometimes fixed games, pocketing money from gamblers. After a group of players conspired to lose the 1919 World Series, eight of them were indicted, acquitted for insufficient evidence, but banned for life from baseball – and forever nicknamed the "Black Sox."

7 1929: Valentine's Day Massacre
This brutal murder of seven of Al Capone's rival gangsters is one of history's most notorious massacres. Capone set up a sting that sent George "Bugsy" Moran's main men to a nearby garage. There, Capone's henchmen, dressed as police officers,

The Chicago White Sox in 1919

lined them up and riddled them with bullets. Seven bushes now mark the spot (at Clark Street and Dickens Avenue).

1942: First atom split
Under the football stands on the campus of the University of Chicago (see pp28–9) Enrico Fermi made history. He supervised the creation of a primitive nuclear reactor and took the first major step in understanding how to build an atomic bomb.

1955: First McDonald's franchise opens
Ray Kroc, a milkshake mixer salesman, changed diets worldwide by convincing Dick and Mac McDonald's to franchise their San Bernadino, California burger stand. The original restaurant in Des Plaines – 15 miles (24 km) west of Chicago – is now a museum.

1983: Harold Washington elected Mayor
Chicago's first African-American Mayor, Washington tragically died of a heart attack shortly into his second term. His accomplishments included the expansion of O'Hare International Airport and the creation of a new central library (see p69).

Top 10 Residents

1 Jean Baptiste Point du Sable
Chicago's first non-native settler was an African-American trader who set up camp around 1779.

2 Jane Addams
This social activist (1860–1935) founded Hull House social center (see p95) and won a Nobel Peace Prize.

3 Carl Sandburg
One of Chicago's nicknames "City of big shoulders," was penned by this author/poet (1878–1967).

4 Al Capone
America's best-known mobster (1899–1947) was Chicago's "Public Enemy Number One" until jailed in 1931 for tax evasion.

5 Ernest Hemingway
Born in Oak Park, this hard-living author (1899–1947) left the suburb of "wide lawns and narrow minds" at age 19.

6 Richard J. Daley
This effective, if corrupt, Chicago mayor (1902–76) served longer than any other.

7 Benny Goodman
Born to poor Russian-Jewish immigrants, jazz great Goodman (1909–86) earned the title "King of Swing."

8 Hugh Hefner
Lothario and founder of Playboy (1926–), whose first issue sold over 50,000 copies.

9 Curtis Mayfield
Soul musician and social activist (1942–99), Mayfield had his first hit For Your Precious Love at age 17.

10 Oprah Winfrey
TV's talk-show darling (1954–) has filmed in Chicago since 1984 and become an honorary native of the city.

Left **333 W. Wacker Drive** Center **Art glass, Auditorium Theatre** Right **860–80 N. Lakeshore Drive**

TOP 10 **Skyscrapers**

1 The Rookery
One of the earliest remaining skyscrapers, this 1888 Chicago landmark (see p70) combines traditional wall-bearing and newer steel frame construction. The latter made it possible for its architects, Burnham and Root, to design an open interior, with office spaces set around a central light well.

2 Auditorium Theatre
Built by Adler and Sullivan in 1889, the ornate Auditorium also originally contained a hotel and office building and had one of the first public air-conditioning systems. The revamped 4,000-seat theater boasts near-perfect acoustics. ✪ 50 E.Congress Pkwy. • Map K5 • For tours call 312-431-2354

3 Monadnock Building
Constructed in two stages, this Loop edifice represents the evolution of skyscraper architecture. The northern half was built in 1891 using solely wall-

Detail of staircase, Monadnock Building

bearing construction, while the southern half was built two years later and incorporated the then emerging steel-frame technology that is still used today (see p72).

4 Reliance Building
The steel skeleton on this 1895-built skyscraper allowed it to be wrapped in glass. It offers an excellent example of the Chicago window, which is characterized by a bay window placed between two narrow, double-hung windows – a signature feature of the Chicago school of architecture. Occupied by the Hotel Burnham (see p116) the interior sports replicas of original features (see p72).

5 860–80 N. Lakeshore Drive
You might think these two highrise apartment buildings (1949–51) look like many others along this tony strip. Actually, the others look like these. German architect Mies van der Rohe perfected the "less is more" approach which so many other architects went on to copy.

6 Marina City
With its twin cylindrical structures (1959–64) on the Chicago River, Marina City is a "city within a city," containing offices, residences, a theater, a grocery store, and more. The apartments start on the 21st floor, affording spectacular views, but their slice-of-pie shape creates some interior decorating challenges.

The Rookery

Sears Tower
This soaring tower, built in 1974 as the headquarters of retailer Sears Roebuck and Co. (who have since moved out), can be seen from almost anywhere in the city. Its Skydeck affords sensational views *(see pp12–13)*.

333 W. Wacker Drive
The graceful curve of this triangular, tinted-glass office building (1983) hugs the Chicago River. The water, together with the changing light and clouds create dynamic reflections: the green and silver lobby continues the shimmering show. Map K3

James R. Thompson Center
From inside the circular atrium of this magnificent 17-story building (1985), a quick glance up is almost dizzying. Take the elevator to the top for an impressive view of the stunning marble rosette on the concourse level *(see p70)*.

Ogilvie Transportation Center
Rising 40 stories in waves of glass and steel is this striking 1996-rebuilt commuter train station (aka the Northwestern Station). Its streamlined façade mimics a vintage luxury train. 500 W. Madison St. • Map J4

Top 10 Architects

1 William Le Baron Jenney
The "father of the skyscraper" (1832–1907) who designed the first all-metal-framed structure in 1885 *(see p34)*.

2 Daniel Burnham
Visionary city planner and architect, Burnham (1846–1912) was the man behind the White City *(see p19)*.

3 William Holabird & Martin Roche
This influential team (Holabird 1854–1923; Roche 1855–1927) developed early Chicago-style skyscrapers including the Marquette Building *(see p72)*.

4 Louis H. Sullivan
The creator (1856–1924) of the "form follows function" doctrine designed according to a building's intended use.

5 Frank Lloyd Wright
Inspired by the wide open spaces of the Midwest, Wright *(see pp30–31)* was the origi-nator of the Prairie style.

6 George Maher
A Prairie School architect (1864–1926) who favored Arts and Crafts motifs.

7 Walter Burley Griffin
Another Prairie–style architect (1876–1937) with a namesake historic district on Chicago's Southside.

8 Ludwig Mies van der Rohe
Minimalist architect (1886–1969) and creator of the modern glass-and-steel box.

9 Bertrand Goldberg
A pupil of Mies van der Rohe who rebelled to produce curvilinear concrete shapes.

10 Harry Weese
A Modernist (1915–98), but one sympathetic to existing buildings of merit.

For other examples of notable Chicago architecture See pp72-3

Left **Exhibit, National Vietnam Veterans Art Museum** Right **Jane Addams Hull House**

Niche Museums

1 National Museum of Mexican Art

The largest Latino museum in the US explores the culture *sin fronteras* (without boundaries), showcasing works from both Mexico and Mexican-American communities. Pre-Columbian ceramics, Day of the Dead candelabras, and prints by such luminaries as Diego Rivera are highlights of the permanent collection. ◎ *1852 W. 19th St • Map B5 • 10am–5pm Tue–Sun • Free • DA*

2 Museum of Broadcast Communications

Dedicated to the culture and history of news and entertainment media, this museum archives over 70,000 radio and television programs and commercials. In addition to watching and hearing vintage tapes, visitors can anchor their own newscast and read from a teleprompter. ◎ *400 N. State St. • Map K3 • Open late spring 2007 • DA*

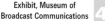

Exhibit, Museum of Broadcast Communications

3 Swedish–American Museum Center

Located in Andersonville, the historic neighborhood of Scandinavian immigrants, this tiny museum's permanent collection of personal items brought over by early settlers is supplemented by temporary exhibitions on Swedish culture. An interactive children's museum on the third floor brings the immigrant journey to life. ◎ *5211 N. Clark St. • Map K2 • 10am–4pm Tue–Fri, 11am–4pm Sat & Sun • Adm.: $4; children, seniors, students $3 • DA*

4 Museum of Holography

The art really jumps out at you in this quirky loft devoted to all kinds of laser-produced 3-D images. Exhibits relating to the technology employed explain how holographs are produced. ◎ *1134 W. Washington St. • Map J4 • 12:30–5pm Wed–Sun • Adm.: $4; children 6–12 $3; under 6 free • DA*

5 The Peace Museum

Art, history, and politics as seen through a pacifist's prism: the Peace Museum houses a 10,000-item collection, including sculpture, banners, and lithographs. Rotating exhibits cover themes such as 20th-century peace movements, the AIDS quilt, and art from Japanese A-bomb survivors. ◎ *100 N. Central Park Ave. • Map B5 • 1–6pm, Thu–Sat, noon–4pm Sun • Donation • No DA*

Work by Jesus Helguera, National Museum of Mexican Art

Hope and Help, International Museum of Surgical Science

Spertus Museum

Here, Judaica in forms ranging from cartoons to ancient Torah scrolls comprise a lively, multi-faceted retelling of Jewish history and culture. The museum's Zell Holocaust Memorial was the first such permanent installation in the US, while the Artifact Center gets kids involved in unearthing the past in a hands-on "archeological dig". ✆ *618 S. Michigan Ave. • Map L6 • 10am–5pm Sun–Thu (7pm Thu), 10am–3pm Fri • Adm., Free Fri • Kosher Café and Children's Center • DA*

DuSable Museum of African-American History

Named for Jean Baptiste Point du Sable, Chicago's first settler (who was of African descent), this museum chronicles the African-American experience. There is a powerful exhibit on slavery, complete with shackles, while temporary displays cover topics such as early black millionaires, African hair art, and the *Kwanzaa* holiday celebration *(see p99)*.

International Museum of Surgical Science

Medicine meets the macabre at this museum, with four floors displaying historic instruments that span 4,000 years of surgery. Murals and sculptures pay tribute to the profession. Stronger stomachs may appreciate the ancient Peruvian skulls showing evidence of early surgical attempts. ✆ *1524 N. Lake Shore Dr. • Map F4 • 10am–4pm, Tue–Sun May–Sep, Tue–Sat Oct–Apr • Adm.: $8; students and seniors $4 • DA*

National Vietnam Veterans Art Museum

Veterans of the Vietnam War, both US and Vietnamese, have contributed to the vast and moving collection of artworks cataloged by this thought-provoking museum. Some 130 artists created 1,000 works in pen, paint, clay, and word testifying to war's horrors *(see p94)*.

Jane Addams Hull House

Nobel Peace Prize-winning social reformer Jane Addams worked her good on Chicago's immigrant population from these two Victorian houses. In addition to her original art and furniture, Hull House stages temporary exhibits relating to the social settlement that brought day care, counseling, and education to the working class *(see p95)*.

Left **Lou Mitchell's** Right **Blackbird**

🔟 Places to Eat

1 Charlie Trotter's

One of Chicago's top gourmet eateries, and one of the nation's best, Charlie Trotter's serves the exquisite and rarefied fare of its eponymous chef. The menu changes daily but expect creations such as venison loin with semolina cake, braised kale, and Niçoise olive *boudin*. Reservations must be made many weeks in advance though a last-minute call often turns up a table due to cancellations *(see p91)*.

2 Ambria

With its Art Nouveau detailing, cozy leather banquettes, and dark woods, Ambria is among the city's most romantic dining options. And the dining experience matches the style here as chef Gabino Soltelino prepares contemporary French meals with a sophisticated understatement. Service is formal and the sommelier is one of the best in Chicago *(see p91)*.

Deep Dish Pizza, Pizzeria Uno

3 Gibson's Steakhouse

Boisterous and convivial, Gibson's exudes a good time. A regular crowd of politicians, sports figures, and conventioneers packs the place nightly. The steakhouse fare is in every way a match to the atmosphere – big and bold. Huge lobster tails vie for attention with large slabs of beef. A reservation is critical, but for a more casual, walk-in

experience try the burgers next door at Hugo's Frog Bar.
Ⓢ 1028 N. Rush St. • Map L2 • 312-266-8999 • $$$$

4 Blackbird

Foodies and the fashion set both agree on Blackbird, an eatery that sports minimalist decor and shoves the tables so close together that eavesdropping becomes part of the experience. Chef Paul Kahan generates the buzz, preparing sophisticated American dishes with French leanings. Menus change seaonally but reservations are perennially a must.
Ⓢ 619 W. Randolph St. • Map J4 • 312-715-0708 • Lunch 11.30am–2pm Mon–Fri, closed Sun • $$$$

5 North Pond Café

Hidden from the road in leafy Lincoln Park, North Pond is a treasure – once you find it. Lodged in an Arts-and-Crafts-style building, the café offers a seasonal menu with an emphasis on produce sourced in the Midwest. Though dinner is the star, lunches of sandwiches, soups, and salads are equally creative and well presented *(see p91)*.

6 Spring

Spring brings the sort of fine cooking you'd expect only to find downtown out to Northside's bohemian Wicker Park. Occupying a former bathhouse, the sunken

For key to price categories **See p75**

feng-shui-inspired interior makes for a chic gourmet experience. The menu features seafood prepared with Asian and French influences and a light approach. ⊗ 2039 W. North Ave. • Map F4 • 1-773-395-7100 • Dinner only, closed Mon • $$$$

Mia Francesca
The hearty, rustic fare of Rome and its surrounding regions distinguishes Mia Francesca from the Italian pack. Large portions and reasonable prices help draw legions of fans to this Wrigleyville rave. A former candy shop, the storefront eatery is casual but stylish with paper-topped tables and black-and-white photos of rural life on the walls. Lines form early and often (see p91).

Frontera Grill
Signature restaurant of chef Rick Bayless, Frontera Grill is credited with bringing authentic regional Mexican food – rather than Tex-Mex taco fare – stateside. Chili-roasted salsas and rich *moles* accompany grilled meats and delicious seafood. Since reservations are only available for parties of more than six, seats in the colorful, folk art-filled room go early as smaller groups try to avoid disappointment (see p83).

Pizzeria Uno
Uno's has been baking deep-dish pizza since 1943 – about as long as Chicagoans have debated whose pie is best. Its version comes several inches deep, filled with cheese and toppings of your choice, truly a meal in one slice. The smallish Victorian brownstone strains under demand, sending the overflow down the street to its spin-off Pizzeria Due. Uno's individual pizza served at lunchtime is a bargain. ⊗ 29 E. Ohio St. • Map L3 • 312-321-1000 • $

Gibson's Steakhouse

Lou Mitchell's
A classic diner in the Loop where the waitresses call you "Honey" and the coffee is bottomless, Lou Mitchell's has been around since 1923. Its trek-worthy meal is breakfast, highlighted by double-yolk eggs and homemade hash browns served in a skillet. Tables turn quickly and the staff doles out free donuts and candy to those waiting on line with good cheer. ⊗ 565 W. Jackson Blvd. • Map J4 • 312-939-3111 • No credit cards • No dinner • $

Unless stated, all restaurants accept credit cards, recommend reservations, and are open for lunch and dinner.

41

Left **Dim Sum at Phoenix** Right **Sushi Bar at Mirai**

Ethnic Eats

Arun's
Distinct from other Thai restaurants in the city, Arun's serves a gourmet version of the spice-and-vegetable driven Asian fare with high quality ingredients and careful presentation. Multi-course fixed-price menus change nightly, and dietary restrictions can be taken into consideration with advance notice. The quiet Thai art-trimmed rooms are conducive to conversation. ✆ 4156 N. Kedzie Ave. • Map B4 • 1-773-539-1909 • Closed Mon, lunch • $$$$$

Pho Xe Tang-Tank
This popular destination in Little Vietnam features several big, round tables for sociable, easy sharing of meals. A vast menu includes traditional dishes such as Bahn Xeo (Vietnamese crispy pancakes) and Pho (noodle soup garnished with heaps of fresh cilantro and basil, with oxtail as an optional extra). Bring your own alcohol. ✆ 4953 N. Broadway • Map B3 • 1-773-878-2253 • Closed Wed • $$

Tiffin

Phoenix
Superior Chinese dim sum, served with a panoramic view of downtown Chicago, garner out-the-door lines for this China-town gem. Dishes emerging from the kitchen are quickly snatched by waiting diners, leading many to ask for a table near it. ✆ 2131 S. Archer Ave. • Map A6 • 312-328-0848 • $$

Mirai Sushi
This hip, two-story eatery carves some of the city's best Japanese sushi. Options include the usual suspects such as tuna and salmon but for the most creative fare sit at the sushi bar, make a special request, and put yourself in the chef's hands. An upstairs lounge serves up sake martinis. ✆ 2020 W. Division St. • Map J1 • 1-773-862-8500 • Closed Sun, lunch • $$$

Ixcapuzalco
This off-the-beaten path, regional Mexican specialist is operated by a protégé of Rick Bayless of Frontera Grill fame (see p41). Foodies head here for the outstanding mole sauces from Oaxaca, which change daily, and top fish, pork, chicken, or beef. ✆ 2919 N. Milwaukee Ave. • Map B4 • 1-773-486-7340 • Closed Tue • $$$$

Tiffin
Locals debate which Indian restaurant along the eatery-and-sari-shop-lined Devon Avenue

(see p52) qualifies as the best. Among them, Tiffin impresses with tender tandoori oven specialties and subtly spiced lentils. More upscale than most of its neighboring competitors, it generates a warm welcome via the enthusiasm of its staff. ◎ 2536 W. Devon Ave. • Map B3 • 1-773-338-2143 • $$

Ann Sather

Locals line up on Sunday mornings at the original Belmont Avenue Ann Sather for plates of oversized, sticky cinnamon rolls. But the Swedish diner makes a more ethnic appeal at lunch and dinner with *limpa* (Swedish rye bread), zesty duck with lingonberries, and hearty Swedish meatballs (see p91).

Ann Sather

Marigold

This Indian restaurant has a modern vibe and the menu reflects multiple regions of India, with vegetarian, seafood and meaty options such as *samosas*, South Indian seafood curry, coriander-crusted halibut with *pakora*-style vegetables, and lamb shank vindaloo. Knowledge-able waiters are on-hand to help curry-challenged diners navigate the menu. ◎ 4832 N. Broadway. • Map B3 • 773-293-4653 • Dinner only, closed Mon • $$

Red Apple

In the heart of Polish Avondale, Red Apple offers budget priced, all-you-can-eat buffets, including dessert and coffee. The diner draws a cross-section of immigrants, artists, students, and the just plain thrifty for authentic dishes such as *pierogi*, borscht, goulash, and stuffed cabbage. ◎ 3121 N. Milwaukee Ave. • Map B4 • 1-773-588-5781 • $

Fogo de Chao

The Sao Paulo owned Fogo de Chao specializes in the all-you-can-eat *churrascaria* tradition of Brazilian barbecue. At your table costumed "gauchos" will carve 15 different cuts of skewer-roasted meats, including filet, rumpsteak, leg of lamb, and pork loin. You can use a plate-side indicator to signal for more or "basta." A lavish salad bar begins every meal. ◎ 661 N. LaSalle St. • Map K2 • 312-932-9330 • Closed Sat & Sun lunch • $$$$

Left **Funky Buddha Lounge** Right **Bin 36**

🔟 Bars & Clubs

La Pomme Rouge
La Pomme boasts two salons: Paradis (paradise) features elegant couches, fireplaces, and a Victorian sideboard; Enfer (hell) has fabric-covered walls, dozens of pillows, and the design decadence of an opium den. In the curtained booths of the main room enjoy the extensive list of champagnes and wines and the posh nibbles, such as caviar. ⊗ *108 W. Kinzie St.* • *Map K3* • *312-245-9555* • *Adm. Fri & Sat*

Whiskey Sky
Nightlife goes sky-high at this intimate club on the 33rd floor of the W. Chicago Lakeshore hotel *(see p117)*. Locals and guests mingle among '70s retro furnishings while soul and light house music provide the beat (though there's no dancing) to a backdrop of stunning views. ⊗ *644 N. Lake Shore Dr.* • *Map M3* • *312-255-4463* • *Free*

Zebra Lounge
An illegal speakeasy during Prohibition, this tiny piano bar has stood the test of time and

Zebra Lounge

competition, packing in loyal revelers nightly. Zebra prints dominate the décor, and martinis are the drink of choice. Singing along with the pianist to show tunes, torch songs, and oldies is expected *(see p83)*.

Funky Buddha Lounge
This favorite is easily identified by the fat, happy Buddha statue outside. Inside, a mixed crowd of urban hipsters and young professionals sip everything from beer to bubbly in the low-ceilinged lounge. As the evening unfolds, the dance floor heats up with clubbers grooving to soul, salsa, hip-hop, R&B, house, rap, and reggae. ⊗ *728 W. Grand Ave.* • *Map K3* • *312-666-1695*

Four
A varied crowd packs the neon-lit two-storey high dancefloor of this off-the-beaten-track club, while local DJs spin techno, rave, and hip-hop. Opt for the signature drink, Four Martini – a blend of four Stoli vodka flavors and a splash of orange juice – while you check out the laser light show under the 4-ft disco ball. ⊗ *1551 W. Division St.* • *Map J1* • *1-773-235-9100* • *Closed Sun & Mon*

Le Passage
Tucked along an alley and down a flight of stairs is the alluring Le Passage. The candlelit, wood-paneled room is divided by gold-wrapped columns.

Unless otherwise stated, bars and clubs are open daily, have a cover charge after 9/10pm, and have DA.

Le Bar

Velvet chairs are free for loung-
ing early on, but later they're
reserved for big spenders. The
dance floor fills up late, with
DJs playing pop remixes. ✆ 937
N. Rush St. • Map L2 • 312-255-0022
• Closed Sun & Mon

Bin 36

This lofty space is a triple
pleasure, with its high-end
restaurant, casual café, and
sociable wine bar. The large, zinc-
topped oval bar is a lively setting
for couples to share conversation
and a cocktail, or for singles to
mingle. "Wine flights" are a
must-try, offering four half-
glasses of different, but related,
wines (see p83).

Le Bar

In the beautiful
Sofitel Hotel (see
p115), a fashionable,
over-30, mixed crowd
fills this lobby lounge
after work, lingering
until the wee hours.
Black-clad servers
dispense martinis with
scrumptious flavors
such as chocolate and
raspberry. ✆ 20 E.
Chestnut St. • Map K2 • 312-
324-4000 • Free

Sonotheque

This small, aluminum-
clad nightclub forgoes
dancing, and instead
focuses on the pure enjoyment of the music. In fact,
every visual aspect here
serves to enhance the fantastic audio system: padded
walls absorb sound, while
the square-cut metal
ceiling tiles diffuse it
throughout the room. The
sonic theme is further
complemented by sleek
steel and cool gray décor.
✆ 1444 W. Chicago Ave. • Map J2 • 312-
226-7600 • Adm. charged some nights
depending on the DJ

J Bar

This sleek, luxurious lounge in
The James hotel offers signature
deconstructed cocktails, such as a
Ketel One martini with a vermouth
and olive lollipop, or the James –
made with Stoli Raz, elderflower
and lime juice, served in a martini
glass coated in a hard, raspberry
candy shell. Modern design, low-
slung lounge seating, candlelit
cocktail tables, and plasma screens
with video art all go to set the
swanky scene. ✆ 610 N Rush St. • Map
L2 • 312-660-7200 • Closed Sun & Mon

Left **Kingston Mines** Right **Green Mill Cocktail Lounge**

Blues & Jazz Joints

Kingston Mines
The largest of Chicago's blues joints, Kingston Mines packs its Lincoln Park locale with students, young professionals, and a broader spectrum of tourists. Two stages provide non-stop musical entertainment from 8pm to near 4am (5am on Saturdays). Acts range from homegrown house bands to national touring headliners. The kitchen serves up beer-sopping barbecue. ⬥ *2548 N. Halsted St. • Map E2 • 1-773-477-4647*

Buddy Guy's Legends
A legend himself, bluesman Buddy Guy operates perhaps the best blues club in the city. The South Loop destination draws a mix of students, tourists, and local fans, particularly when Guy himself headlines. The place gets so packed that aisles are marked on the flooring and monitored by bouncers who make sure standing-room-only patrons keep them clear *(see p96)*. ⬥ *754 S. Wabash Ave. • Map L5 • 312-427-1190*

B.L.U.E.S.
Among Chicago's many blues clubs, B.L.U.E.S feels the most like a Southern juke joint. Chalk it up to the narrow confines, loud sounds, and sweaty dancers. The club is across the street from the popular Kingston Mines, but it's a better choice for older, more musically versed blues fans. Better yet, why not stop into both! ⬥ *2519 N. Halsted St. • Map E2 • 1-773-528-1012*

Green Mill Cocktail Lounge
A former Prohibition era speakeasy, Uptown's landmark Green Mill is a vintage treasure with a sweeping curved bar, vinyl booths, fading murals, and an authentic air of Chicago's gangster past. The city's premier jazz talents like Kurt Elling and Patricia Barber regularly play gigs here and Uptown Poetry Slam feature every sunday. It's out of the way but every cabbie knows how to get there. ⬥ *4802 N. Broadway • Map E2 • 1-773-878-5552 • Limited DA*

House of Blues
Folk art and exotic architectural remnants festoon the funky House of Blues. The vast 1500-seat concert hall presents a variety of national touring acts from hard rock to hip hop in addition to blues. The Sunday gospel

Andy's Jazz Club

Unless otherwise stated all venues are open daily, charge admission, and have DA.

brunch with seatings from 9:30am to noon is a must. ✆ 329 N. Dearborn St. • Map K3 • 312-923-2000

The Velvet Lounge
The new location for Chicago saxophonist Fred Anderson's Velvet Lounge offers a less worn-down atmosphere than its former home on S. Indiana Ave., where a wide range of jazz greats played since 1982. However, some of the old features have been retained, such as the chandeliers. Now regulars and an increasing array of new fans populate the club. Sunday nights see regular jam sessions (see p.96).

Rosa's
Though off-the-beaten club path, the family-owned Rosa's is beloved citywide for its support of local artists such as blues harpist Sugar Blue and the genuine welcome by its owners, Tony Mangiullo and his mother Rosa. The latter sometimes cooks for the patrons of this simple tavern. ✆ 3420 W. Armitage Ave. • Map E4 • 1-773-342-0452 • Closed Sun & Mon • www.rosaslounge.com

Green Dolphin St.
This slick Northside jazz club offers some of the city's best sight-lines. Named for a jazz standard, Green Dolphin encompasses both a separate fine dining restaurant and an equally spacious showroom that also serves casual café fare. On the musical bill expect the sorts of ensembles that can audibly fill the space, such as big bands and Latin groups. ✆ 2200 N. Ashland Ave. • Map D2 • 1-773-395-0066 • Closed Mon • www.jazzitup.com

Blue Chicago
Popular with tourists, Blue Chicago in River North operates two clubs located two blocks

Buddy Guy's Legends

apart. Seats at both venues are few and far between, so come early if you need one, or be prepared to dance. The admission charge covers both clubs, which encourages bar hopping. ✆ 536 N. Clark St. & 736 N. Clark St. • Map K2 • 312-661-0100 • Closed Mon & Sun respectively • www.blueschicago.com

Andy's Jazz Club
With its musical program-ming that begins at lunchtime and continues into the evening, Andy's fills a void for those jazz fans who can't hold out for the late-night headliners. Prime perches are much sought after at the horseshoe-shaped bar in the no-fuss River North club. ✆ 11 E. Hubbard St. • Map K3 • 312-642-6805

Left **Steppenwolf Theatre Co.** Right **Gene Siskel Film Center**

![10] **Arts Venues**

Civic Opera House
This imposing Art Deco building is largely devoted to performances by the Lyric Opera. Each year (September through March), the company stages work by everyone from Wagner to Gilbert and Sullivan. Touring classical dance troops and musicals fill the off-season bill.
🔇 *20 N. Wacker Dr. • Map J4 •* www.civicoperahouse.com

Symphony Center
While visiting orchestras, lecturers, and jazz artists feature on its program, this center is first and foremost the home of the Chicago Symphony Orchestra. The complex holds a main stage, recital hall, and a bar-restaurant named Rhapsody (see p75).
🔇 *220 S. Michigan Ave. • Map L6 • www.cso.org*

Steppenwolf Theatre Co.
Founded in 1974 in a church basement, Steppenwolf has gained acclaim based on the fame of its ensemble, which includes actor John Malkovich. Though the company has moved upscale to a specially built theater in Lincoln Park, it is still distinguished by raw emotion and edgy productions. 🔇 *1650 N. Halsted St. • Map E2 • www.steppenwolf.org*

Goodman Theatre
One of Chicago's leading theater companies, the Goodman frequently spins off

Court Theatre

productions to Broadway in New York and has earned a Tony award, the theater community's highest, for its efforts. Noted productions include dramas by Eugene O'Neill and August Wilson and an annual version of Charles Dickens' *A Christmas Carol.* 🔇 *170 N. Dearborn St. • Map K3 • www.goodman-theatre.org*

Chicago Shakespeare Theater
This Navy Pier venue presents a dynamic space for Shakespeare's repertory. The 510-seat courtyard design is inspired by the original layout in traditional playhouses of the Bard's day. Visiting non-Shakespeare productions take over after the company's September-to-April season.
🔇 *800 E. Grand Ave. • Map L3 • www.chicagoshakes.com*

Second City
Since 1959, Chicago's famed Second City comedy troupe has launched such comic lights as John Belushi, Mike Myers, and Bill Murray. Actors improvize their lines in a series of skits connected by a current events theme on the cabaret-style main stage. Reservations are a must.
⊗ 1616 N. Wells St. • Map K2
• www.secondcity.com

Court Theatre
This theater traces its roots to three Molière productions performed at the University of Chicago in 1955. The Court still mounts many classics, but it varies its seasons with musicals like Guys and Dolls and literary adaptations such as James Joyce's The Dead. ⊗ 5535 S. Ellis Ave. • Map E5 • www.courttheatre.org

Old Town School of Folk Music
Since the 1950s the Old Town School has brought world and homegrown folk music performers to Chicago. Its new home in Lincoln Square opened in 1998 with a concert by Joni Mitchell, though you're more likely to catch a women's ensemble from Mali and contemporary folkies such as Patty Larkin. ⊗ 4544 N. Lincoln Ave. • Map E3 • www.oldtownschool.org

Lookingglass Theatre
In 1988, eight Northwestern University students founded Lookingglass, a bold company incorporating dance, circus arts, and live music in its original theatrical productions. Celebrity

Old Town School of Folk Music

membership (including Friends actor David Schwimmer) and Broadway bound, award-winning shows have furthered this company's stardom. ⊗ 821 N. Michigan Ave. • Map L2
• www.lookingglasstheatre.org

Gene Siskel Film Center
Tiny by cineplex standards, the Gene Siskel Film Center screens films from the silent era onwards. Cineastes will rave about the cushy rocking chairs, excellent sightlines, and art gallery as well as foreign, independent and experimental films rarely shown elsewhere.
⊗ 164 N. State St. • Map K2
• www.siskelfilmcenter.com

For information on entertainment in Chicago See p109.

49

Left **Taste of Chicago** Center **Venetian Night** Right **Chicago Gospel Music Festival**

🔟 Festivals & Events

Chicago Blues Festival
The raucous weekend-long Blues Festival kicks off summer in Chicago. An estimated 750,000 listeners converge on Grant Park for the world's largest free blues event. The main stage line-up spans traditional bluesmen like Honey Boy Edwards, jazz interpreters such as Mose Allison, and blues-inflected popsters like Bonnie Raitt. Smaller side stages offer a more intimate audience experience. ✪ *Map L6* • *312-744-3315* • *Late May–early Jun*

Chicago Summer Neighborhood Festivals
Chicago is a city of neighborhoods with upwards of 100 neighborhood festivals to prove it. Virtually every summer weekend features an event or three ranging from the gay-oriented North Halsted Market Days to the ethnic Korean Street Festival. ✪ *312-744-3315* • *May–Sep*

Neighborhood festival in Chinatown

Chicago Gospel Music Festival
For three days Grant Park resounds with stirring choirs and impassioned soloists. Headliners have included R&B-star-turned-Memphis-preacher, Al Green. ✪ *Map L6* • *312-744-3315* • *Early Jun*

Old Town Art Fair
This 50-year-old fair installs 250 artist booths along Old Town's historic and leafy lanes. The artwork is supplemented by food vendors, kids' entertainment, and garden tours. ✪ *1763 N. Park Ave.* • *Off Map* • *312-337-1938* • *www.oldtown triangle.com* • *Jun* • *Adm.*

Ravinia Festival
The summer home of the Chicago Symphony Orchestra, Ravinia stages concerts (classical, jazz, and pop) in suburban Highland Park. Sheltered seats are available but it's more fun to pack a picnic and join the crowds on the lawn. ✪ *Off Map* • *1-847-266-5100* • *www.ravinia.org* • *Jun–Sep* • *Adm.*

Taste of Chicago
Chicago's signature foods including deep dish pizza star during the nearly two-week long Taste. Musical entertainers, a carnival with rides, and cooking demonstrations entertain at the sprawling Grant Park event. ✪ *Map L6* • *312-744-3315* • *Late Jun–early Jul*

Venetian Night
On this night, boat owners dress up their ships and form a

Unless otherwise indicated all festivals and events are free and have DA.

Chicago Air & Water Show

festive marine parade that culminates with fireworks over the lake. For the best views try Monroe Harbor at the lakefront. ✆ 312-744-3315 • Late Jul/early Aug

Chicago Air & Water Show
This massive display of military power features historic aircraft flybys, a staged amphibious attack, and precision flying teams. Prime beachfront viewing spots are from Oak Street to Montrose Beach. ✆ 312-744-3315 • Mid-Aug

Chicago Jazz Festival
Just as the Blues Fest ushers in summer, the smaller Jazz Fest caps it. Music fans are drawn to Grant Park for free concerts by a range of jazz greats like Branford Marsalis and Roy Hargrove.
✆ Map L6 • 312-744-3315 • Late Aug/early Sep (inc. Labor Day weekend)

Magnificent Mile Holiday Lights Festival
Merchants mark the start of the holiday season by lighting the shops, lampposts, and trees along Michigan Avenue. The parade and fireworks above the Chicago River on the Saturday night before Thanksgiving warrant braving the inevitable chill.
✆ Map L2 • Mid Nov–end Dec

Top 10 Sports Teams & Events

Chicago Cubs
Despite the Cubbies' losing streak, their baseball games are often sell-outs (see p85).

Chicago White Sox
The White Sox are renowned for their top-quality baseball. ✆ 312-674-1000 • www. whitesox.com • Apr–Sep

Chicago Bears
A football team generating rabid fans and tailgate picnics on Soldier Field (see p12). ✆ Ticketmaster 312-559-1212 • www. chicagobears.com • Sep–Dec

Chicago Bulls
Their basketball just hasn't been the same since superstar Michael Jordan left. ✆ 312-455-4000 • www.bulls.com • Oct–Apr

Chicago Blackhawks
NHL ice hockey team sharing the United Center (see p13) with the Bulls. ✆ 312-455-7000 • www. chicagoblackhawks.com • Oct–Apr

Arlington Park
Thoroughbreds race just north of Chicago. ✆ 1-847-385-7500 • www.arlingtonpark.com • May–Sep

Chicago Fire
Many local Latino soccer fans support the Fire. ✆ 1-888-657-3473 • www.chicago-fire.com • Apr–Oct

Chicago Wolves
AHL's Wolves have a better playoff record than NHL's Blackhawks. ✆ 1-800-843-9658 • www. chicagowolves.com • Oct–May

Chicago Marathon
40,000 entrants run through the city. ✆ 312-904-9800 • www. chicagomarathon.com • Oct

Chicago Triathlon
Over 6,000 run, bike, and swim in this one-dayer. ✆ www. chicagotriathlon.com • Aug

For information on Chicago Events See p109

Left **Mi Barrio Taqueria, Pilsen** Right **Mural, Lincoln Square**

🔟 Ethnic Neighborhoods

Pilsen

Named after a city in the former Czech Republic, whose immigrants settled here in the mid-1800s, this neighborhood now claims the Midwest's largest Mexican community. It's anchored by the Mexican Fine Arts Center Museum *(see p38)* and animated by street vendors, mariachi music, and Mexican restaurants. Vibrant outdoor murals and mosaics portray Mexican culture and history. 🌐 *Map B5*

Avondale

In the early 20th century, menial jobs at Avondale's local factories and brickyards attracted many hard-working Polish immigrants. Today, the area also has many Hispanics, but it's still known as Little Warsaw because Chicago holds the largest concentration of Poles outside the Polish capital. Milwaukee Avenue and the neighboring streets also abound with bakeries, bookstores, delis, and a Polish Museum. 🌐 *Map B4*

Building detail in Chinatown

Devon Avenue

Chicagoans who crave cheap, authentic Indian food head north to Devon Avenue in Rogers Park. Nineteenth-century English settlers named it after Devonshire, but since the 1960s, it's been a thriving Indian community, mingled with Russian, Greek, Syrian, and Jewish enclaves. From colorful saris to Indian videos to savory curried meats, it's almost like being in Delhi. 🌐 *Map B3*

Andersonville

Amid a mix of Middle-Eastern and Asian cultures, the late-19th-century Swedish heritage here still makes its presence felt with billowing yellow and blue flags, Swedish bakeries and shops, and the Swedish-American Museum *(see p38)*. Adding to the minority mix is an increasing gay population – more laid-back than Boys Town *(see p85)* – evident in a number of trendy, gay-owned restaurants. 🌐 *Map B3*

Little Italy, Taylor Street

The rich smells of garlic, basil, and baking bread waft from restaurants that line one of Chicago's oldest southern Italian neighborhoods. Though the streets have fewer Italians than when immigrants arrived in the late 19th century, you'll still see Italians chatting on street corners and toting groceries from Italian markets. 🌐 *Map G6*

Heart of Italy

Northern Italians settled here in the 1920s, and some Chicagoans argue that this west side neighborhood is actually

 For Ethnic Eats **See pp42–3**

Little Italy

Lincoln Square

Beer, bratwursts, and grainy rye breads are order of the day in this bustling German enclave, where a 96-ft (29-m) outdoor mural depicts a rural German village. The hub of activity is a relatively small strip of Lincoln Avenue, between Lawrence and Western Avenues. The area maintains Old World charm with its German shops, delicatessens, bakeries, and an old-fashioned apothecary. ◈ Map B3

the real Little Italy. It has a handful of authentic Italian restaurants and delis, as well as the Taste of Italy festival, held over Father's Day weekend every June. ◈ Map B5

Chinatown

An ornate arched gateway at Wentworth Avenue signals your entrance to this distinctly Chinese neighborhood. Asians and non-Asians alike flock to aroma-filled dim-sum restaurants that serve a mouthwatering selection of dumplings, duck, egg rolls, and other delicacies. Shops sell everything from lanterns to delicate tea sets and mysterious Chinese herbs (see p94).

Uptown

The eclectic Uptown neighborhood is nicknamed the United Nations for its ethnic diversity. Along Argyle Street, it's called Little Saigon for its predominantly Vietnamese flavor. Inexpensive restaurants serve thinly sliced beef, tangy soups, and shrimp crêpes. Though the area is absolutely fascinating to explore, it's really not advisable to walk through Uptown late at night. ◈ Map B3

Bridgeport

First called Hardscrabble, this South Side neighborhood is one of the city's oldest, being settled in the 1830s by Irish laborers who came to help build the Illinois-Michigan Canal. Bridgeport still has a mostly Irish population, and has bred five Chicago mayors, including Richard J. Daley (see p35) and his son, Richard M. Daley. The area centerpiece is US Cellular Field (formerly Comiskey Park), home ground of the Chicago White Sox (see p51). ◈ Map B5

Next Pages **Mexican Mural, Pilsen**

Left **Museum of Science & Industry** Right **Visitors viewing animals, Lincoln Park Zoo**

🔟 Kids' Chicago

1 Chicago Children's Museum

The engrossing, imaginative exhibits here emphasize doing – be it digging up a dinosaur bone or designing a water channel. A central, three-story rope tunnel immediately snares the attention of older visitors, though there are age-appropriate attractions for infants to pre-teens. If this place can't exhaust the younger set's energies, nowhere can.
❀ *700 E. Grand Ave. • Map L3 • Open 10am–5pm Tue–Sun (to 8pm Thu & Sat) • www.chichildrensmuseum.org • Adm.*

2 Lincoln Park Zoo

Free admission encourages repeat visits to the Lincoln Park Zoo *(see pp24–5)*. Many exhibits, including the working Farm in the Zoo and the Children's Zoo, allow kids to pet the animals. In summer a motorized "train" makes a scenic loop around the park, while on the pond, swan-shaped paddleboats float among the ducks.

3 Navy Pier

Kids make a beeline for Navy Pier's old-fashioned carnival rides including a 10-story Ferris Wheel and musical carousel . The ships that line the docks, from sleek, tall-masted schooners to powerful motor boats will also grab their attention. All the restaurants

here are family friendly, and even the sculptures that line the Pier in summer are designed to withstand climbers *(see pp20–21)*.

4 Elevated Trains

Chicago's elevated trains (the El) provide an inexpensive roofline tour of the city. The Brown Line in particular warrants riding en famille from Chicago Station south over the Chicago River and around the Loop, threading between the massive buildings of the financial district. Sit in the first row of the front car for an exciting view of the city ahead of you *(see p108)*.

5 Shedd Aquarium

Upon arrival, head straight for the Oceanarium to watch the thrilling dolphin and beluga whale show. Staff trainers frequently choose children in the audience to help them reward the marine mammals

Shedd Aquarium with a snack after each trick. At the daily Tide Pool Touch and reptilian Animal Encounters kids can indulge their urge to lay hands on the critters *(see pp22–3)*.

6 Westfield North Bridge Mall

Level 3 of this tony Michigan Avenue mall is primarily devoted to children's retailers including clothiers Oilily Children, Benetton Kids, The Children's Place, and

Hello Kitty! specialist, Sanrio. Across the hall from the Lego store, the Lego Construction Zone sets out Lego bricks for play. The fourth floor food court sells kid-favored foods like hot dogs and pizza. ◎ *520 N. Michigan Ave. • Map L2 • Open 10am–8pm Mon–Sat, 11am–7pm Sun*

Navy Pier

Emerald City Theatre Company

In Chicago there's a theater company for every demographic and Emerald City is its troupe devoted to young audiences. Expect lively productions such as *Where the Wild Things Are* as well as holiday season shows in weekend-only midday matinees at Lincoln Park's Apollo Theater. ◎ *2540 N. Lincoln Ave. • Map E3 • Open Oct–May • 773-529-2690 • www.emeraldcitytheatre.com • Adm.*

Museum Of Science & Industry

Though this museum dazzles kids and adults alike with its submarine ship and replica coal mine, it's The Idea Factory that's designed just for Junior. With the pulling of gears and shifting of knobs, kids experiment through play with balance, construction, magnetism, and more. A current-fed waterway encourages boat building. Arrive early on weekends or expect to have to wait for access *(see pp16–19).*

Wrigley Field

A baseball lover's park, Wrigley is a small and intimate stadium that's far less intimidating for children than many larger stadia *(see p85).* A ticket to anywhere in the grandstand allows you to walk around and get to the rooftop terrace with its great views: the outfield stands can get rowdy, but a neighboring family section bans the beer that fuels the "bleacher bums."

The Café at American Girl Place

Vendor of dolls with educational aims, American Girl Place feeds its fantasy world, literally, in a café where dolls are welcome in clip-to-the-table chairs. Lunch leans to simple crowd-pleasers like tomato soup, while dinner supplies standards like chicken potpie. In between, the imaginative tea proffers chocolate pudding in a flowerpot or heart-shaped sandwiches. Reservations recommended *(see p82).*

Left **Endo Exo, Armitage Avenue** Center **State Street Store** Right **Bloomingdale's Home Store**

🔟 Shopping Destinations

1 State Street
A slew of chain stores line this legendary street *(see p70)*, but it's the two old-time department stores that make it unique. The former Marshall Field's, now Macy's *(see p74)*, here since 1907, has merchandise to satisfy every wealthy woman's needs. At Filene's Basement the prices are lower, but the variety is still extensive *(see p74)*.

2 Magnificent Mile
Some 450 stores make this stretch of North Michigan Avenue one of the world's retail meccas. Besides sophisticated designer boutiques, there are malls (each with high-end department stores); and big-name chain and flagship stores *(see pp26–7)*.

3 Oak Street
If you have to ask how much it costs, you should probably plan on just window-shopping along

Prairie Avenue Bookshop

this stretch of Chicago's upper-crust Gold Coast. Boutiques here sell designer wear, accessories, and shoes fit for a Paris runway – and include some shops exclusive to Chicago such as Tessuti (menswear) and Designs by Ming (custom clothing design). ◉ *Borders: N. Michigan Ave. & Rush St. • Map L1*

4 Jeweler's Row
This small strip in the Loop boasts a large number of jewelers that sell everything from discount diamonds to top-of-the-range gems. The Jeweler's Center at the beautiful 1912 Mallers Building *(see p74)* packs about 50 wholesale and retail jewelers and appraisers into 13 floors.

5 Bucktown Neighborhood
Once a hot-spot for starving artists, Bucktown and adjacent Wicker Park are now gentrified locales brimming with vintage clothes stores, edgy music shops, high-style designer boutiques, and antiques importers. ◉ *Borders: Fullerton Ave. to North Ave. & Kennedy Expressway to Western Ave. • Map B4*

6 Broadway Antique Market
An old-time movie palace marquee indicates the 1939 building that houses this market. With 85 dealers stocking artwork, jewelry, clothing, and more in styles such as Arts and Crafts, Art Deco, and Victorian, you're sure to find something that pleases. ◉ *6130 N. Broadway • Map E2 • Open 11am–7pm, Mon–Sat, 11am–6pm Sun • DA*

Prairie Avenue Bookshop

It's fitting that a city known for its architecture has one of the best architectural bookstores in the world. Besides carrying a range of 17,000 new and 7,000 out-of-print titles, the store is also appointed with furniture designed by Frank Lloyd Wright, Mies van der Rohe, and Le Corbusier (see p74).

Chicago Architecture Foundation Shop

Located in the historic Santa Fe Center (see p72), this shop is part of the CAF's ArchiCenter, which also puts on exhibitions and runs city tours. Browse the shop for architecture and design-related books; art-glass panels and lamps in Frank Lloyd Wright designs; desk gadgets; and desirable kitchen gizmos.
⊗ 224 S. Michigan Ave. • Map L6 •
Open 9:30am–6pm daily • DA

Bloomingdale's Home & Furniture Store

This store's lovingly restored 1913 Moorish-style building is an attraction in its own right. Inside there's a sleek, four-level atrium with home decor departments that sell everything from high-thread-count bedding to chic cookware and top-quality furniture.
⊗ 600 N. Wabash Ave. • Map K3
• Opening times vary • DA

Armitage Avenue

This tree-lined street in Lincoln Park (see p85) is a favorite for those who are seeking out-of-the-ordinary clothing, home decor, bath and body products – and don't mind spending more to get it. Have patience finding a parking spot on weekends; once you're in, just shop-hop from one adorable boutique to the next.

Top 10 Souvenirs

1 Frango Mints
Marshall Field's/Macy's (see p74) doesn't make these melt-away mint chocolates anymore, but still sells them by the box-full.

2 Blues & Jazz CDs
CDs by Chicago music legends are on sale at the Water Tower Visitor Information Center (see p109).

3 Cows on Parade
Mini versions of the highly decorated cows from 1999s "Cows on Parade" display are sold at the ArchiCenter store.

4 Art poster
See the real thing, then buy a copy at the extensive Art Institute gift shop (see p8).

5 Michael Jordan Jersey
No longer a Bull, but he's still a star. Buy Jordan's merchandise at United Center's (see p13) Fandemonium store.

6 Cubs baseball cap
Head to the Tribune Tower (see p27) gift shop for caps of the Major League team owned by the Chicago Tribune.

7 Art glass
Get a little Prairie style with a replica Frank Lloyd Wright art-glass panel from the Chicago Architecture Foundation store.

8 Chicago mugs
The Chicago Historical Society (see p86) sells mugs depicting the faces of famous local residents like Al Capone.

9 Sue skeleton
Sue, the world's largest T. rex skeleton is far less menacing in mini model form from the Field Museum (see p14).

10 Chicago snowglobe
Recall Chicago winters with a city skyline snowglobe from Accent Chicago in the Water Tower Place mall (see p26).

For more on shopping in Chicago See pp74, 82, 88, 102, 113.

Left **Scene from** *The Relic*, set at the Field Museum Right **Andy Garcia in** *Hero*, Drake Hotel

Film Locations

Daley Center & Plaza
Daley Plaza *(see p73)* with its famed Picasso sculpture was the setting for a sensational chase scene in cult movie classic *The Blues Brothers* (1980). Stars John Belushi and Dan Aykroyd, playing ex-criminal brothers, dramatically crash their car through the center's plate-glass windows, specially installed for the filming, as the authorities hopelessly attempt to stop them.

James R. Thompson Center
In *Running Scared* (1986) Billy Crystal and Gregory Hines are Chicago police pals planning early retirement, but first they must thwart a drug kingpin and stay alive. The final chase scene takes place in the Thompson Center *(see p37)* where the two swap wisecracks while swinging on ropes through the airy atrium, shooting out glass elevators, and ultimately triumphing.

The Art Institute of Chicago
The consummate high school comedy *Ferris Bueller's Day Off* (1986) stars Matthew Broderick,

Exterior of State of Illinois Center as featured in *Running Scared*

who skips school and takes his girlfriend (Mia Sara) and best friend (Paul Ruck) on an action-packed Chicago day. At the Art Institute, Broderick and Sara kiss in front of a window designed by Chagall, while Ruck stares intensely at *A Sunday on La Grande Jatte –1884 (see p8).*

Union Station
Elliott Ness (Kevin Costner) brings down Chicago gangster Al Capone (Robert DeNiro) in the true story *The Untouchables* (1987). In one unforgettable scene, a shoot-out on a Union Station staircase causes a mother to lose her grip on her baby carriage, which bounces in slow motion down the stairs, saved at the last moment by Ness's partner.
210 S. Canal St. • Map J5

While You Were Sleeping at the Randolph El Station

Drake Hotel
In feel-good film *Hero* (1992) John Bubber (Andy Garcia) dupes the public into thinking he's a hero. Feeling

guilty, he resolves to jump off a window ledge at The Drake *(see p115)*. Reality interrupted the filming when guests arrived for a party at the hotel. Director Stephen Frears protested so violently, he almost got arrested.

A scene from *Chain Reaction* on Michigan Avenue Bridge

The Hilton Chicago

Wrongly accused and convicted of murder, Dr. Richard Kimble (Harrison Ford) dodges the authorities led by Tommy Lee Jones to prove his innocence in *The Fugitive* (1993). He winds up in a pulse-pounding chase through this grand hotel *(see p116)* onto its roof, down its elevator shaft, and into the hotel's laundry room.

Randolph El Station

The El tracks are an apt symbol of hard-working Chicago, and they feature significantly in the romantic comedy *While You Were Sleeping* (1995). Sandra Bullock plays an El station clerk who falls in love with a handsome commuter. He tumbles off the platform, Bullock saves his life, and comedy and romance ensue. Map L4

Field Museum

Scare-fest *The Relic* (1997) starred Penelope Ann Miller and Tom Sizemore as researchers trying to stop a murderous monster before it killed again. Many interior scenes were shot on replica sets but were near-perfect matches to the real museum *(see pp14–15)*.

Michigan Avenue Bridge

Chain Reaction (1996) sees Keanu Reeves as a science student at the University of Chicago *(see pp28–9)* who is framed for murder. In a nail-biting chase scene, he tries to escape by running up the Michigan Avenue Bridge *(see p27)* as it's raised.

Wrigley Building

In *Road to Perdition* (2002), Tom Hanks is Michael Sullivan, an Irish gangster living in 1930s Chicago. After his wife and young son are murdered, he flees town with his older son. In seeking a safe refuge, they enter a hotel, the exterior of which is the beautiful Wrigley Building *(see p27)*. However, the interior scenes were actually filmed at The Hilton Chicago.

Left Blues Festival, Grant Park Right Gold Coast seen from Oak Street Beach

Parks & Beaches

Millennium & Grant parks

As well as a center for world-class art, music, architecture and landscape design, the 24-acre (10-ha) Millennium Park offers winter ice skating, interactive public art, al fresco dining and free classical music concerts. Together with the adjoining 19th century Grant Park, which hosts many of the city's varied and vibrant festivals *(see pp50–51)*, it constitutes one of the finest, user-friendly green spaces in Chicago *(see p71)*.

Lincoln Park

The greenway Lincoln Park stretches from North Avenue up to Hollywood Avenue, a recreational apron between lakefront and housing. In Chicago's infancy, the southern portion of the park was a cemetery for Civil War dead, later exhumed and interred elsewhere to make way for the park. Now it's the North Side's counterpart to Grant Park. Popular attractions such as Lincoln Park Zoo *(see pp24–5)*, the Lincoln Park Conservatory *(see p86)*, and Peggy Notebaert Nature Museum *(see p85)* supplement the beaches, harbors, playing fields, and bike paths. ◈ Map F3

The Republic, Jackson Park

North Avenue Beach

Chicago's most populist beach, North Avenue Beach attracts a broad range of urban-dwellers. Its lively ocean-liner-shaped bathhouse (which includes umbrella rentals, shower rooms, snack vendors, and a rooftop restaurant) makes it particularly family friendly. Rows of beach volleyball courts draw teams often made up of impromptu players, and a seasonal outdoor gym welcomes day use *(see p86)*.

Oak Street Beach

At the foot of the tony Gold Coast shopping lane, Oak Street Beach reflects its environs. Though just next to North Avenue Beach, you won't see many children here. With its emphasis on flesh and flash, Oak Street is usually filled with toned bodies and tiny bikinis. Still, the crescent-shaped strand is the closest beach to the Magnificent Mile *(see pp26–7)* and makes a great place to stop and dip your toes after some serious shopping. ◈ Map L1

Jackson Park

Laid out by the famed landscape designer Frederick Law Olmsted for the 1893 World's Columbian Exposition, Jackson Park, along with its Museum of Science & Industry *(see pp16–19)*, is among the few developments still remaining from that World's Fair. The Southside park includes a Japanese garden with waterfalls,

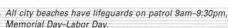

Bathhouse, North Avenue Beach

colorful lanterns, and a bird sanctuary on an island in a peaceful lagoon. ⦾ *Map F6*

Burnham Park
Designed by and named for city planner Daniel Burnham, Burnham Park is the city's green lawn rolling south from Museum Campus *(see p92)* to Hyde Park. Like Lincoln and Grant parks, it is charted by the lakefront bike path, but unlike its northern counterparts Burnham Park's section isn't overrun, making this south-leg journey far more enjoyable. Along the way you'll find basketball courts and beaches. The return trip north provides city skyline panoramas. ⦾ *Map C6*

Montrose Beach
Stretching nearly to Wilson Avenue, Montrose is spacious where downtown beaches are jammed. Convenient for swimmers, this North Side spot includes a changing house and shower facilities. The vast playing fields wedged between the sand and Lake Shore Drive are the domain of Hispanic soccer clubs: on weekends their numbers draw Latin food and balloon vendors. Look for kayak rentals that launch here in summer. ⦾ *Map C3*

Foster Beach
Near the northern end of the lakefront bike path, Foster Beach proves a timely spot to cool off. There's a snack bar, and the nearby picnic tables and grills draw family crowds. A beachside basketball court hosts lively free-for-all games to which only the talented should apply. ⦾ *Map B3*

Olive Park
A pocket-sized park just beside Navy Pier *(see pp20–21)*, Olive Park makes great strolling grounds. Jutting into Lake Michigan just off Ohio Street, it provides skyline views similar to Navy Pier's though without the tourist mobs. Quiet and out of the way, this is one of the city's most romantic parks. ⦾ *Map M2*

Washington Square
Opposite the historic Newberry Library, Washington Square is a prime plot of Gold Coast for resting tired feet and gazing at the handsome 1892 building. The park's ample benches tend to draw bookish sorts and picnicking office workers at lunchtime. ⦾ *Map K2*

For information on bike rental **See p108**

Left **Chicago Botanic Garden** Center **Church window, Historic Pullman District** Right **IIT**

🔟 Sights off the Beaten Track

1 Garfield Park Conservatory
Beneath glass-domed roofs, flora from around the world thrives in spacious greenhouses. Information panels give the low-down as you stroll through the conservatory's six indoor areas that include a Children's Garden and the Sweet House (containing plants such as cacao, sugar cane, etc). ◈ 300 N. Central Park Ave. • Map B5 • 312-746-5100 • El station: Conservatory-Central Park Dr. (green line) • Open 9am–5pm daily, Thu 9am–8pm • Free • DA

2 Chicago Botanic Garden
About 25 miles (40 km) north of Chicago, this attraction comprises 385 acres (155 ha) of natural habitats and beautifully landscaped gardens. Some of the most popular are the romantic Rose Garden, the tranquil island-based Japanese Garden, and the charming English Walled Garden. ◈ 1000 Lake Cook Rd. Glencoe • 1-847-835-5440 • Map A1 • Metra station: Glencoe • Open 8am–sunset daily • Adm. • DA

Grosse Point Lighthouse, Evanston

3 Historic Pullman District
This industrial town was conceived in the 1880s by railroad magnate George Pullman for his workers. The planned utopia had apartments, shops, a hospital, and a hotel, but failed after a strike in 1894, when a decrease in wages made rents unaffordable. ◈ Map C6 • Metra Station: Pullman/111th St. • Visitor Center: 11141 S. Cottage Grove Ave., open 11am–3pm Tue–Sun • 1-773-785-8901 • DA

4 Illinois Institute of Technology (IIT)
In 1940, Ludwig Mies van der Rohe planned the campus of this new university. He also designed around 20 of the buildings, which demonstrate his design philosophies. Stop by the on-campus visitor center for information and docent-guided or self-guided tours. ◈ 3201 S. State St. (Visitor Center) • Map C5 • 312-567-3000 • El station: 35th-Bronzeville-IIT (green line) • Tours $5 • DA

5 Sheridan Road
This lakefront road's low speed limit is perfect for gawping at the palatial, architecturally diverse homes that line it as you drive north to Evanston and beyond. Art buffs might like to stop at the Evanston Art Center at Harley Clarke House – one of the oldest and largest community visual art centers in Illinois. ◈ From Rogers Park to Lake Bluff • Map B2 • Evanston Art Center, 2603 N. Sheridan Rd., 847-475-5300, open 10am–10pm Mon–Thu, 10am–1pm Fri & Sat, 1–4pm Sun, Free

Bronzeville

A bronze memorial at Martin Luther King, Jr. Drive and 35th Street honors the journey many African-Americans made to this neighborhood as they fled the oppression of the South in the early 20th century. Nearby, sidewalk plaques celebrate local luminaries. Chicago's answer to Harlem offers jazz and blues in its clubs, graceful mansions aplenty, and lots of fine soul food. ⬗ *Map C5 • El station: 35th-Bronzeville-IIT (green line)*

Baha'i Temple

This exquisite white structure is one of eight temples of the Baha'i faith worldwide. Its nine doors symbolize how people can come to God from any direction. At night, spotlights enhance its ethereal beauty. ⬗ *100 Linden Ave, Wilmette • Map A1 • El station: Linden Ave • Visitors' Center open 10am–8pm daily (Oct–May to 5pm); Temple open 7am–10pm daily • 1-847-853-2300 • Free • DA*

Historic Long Grove

Thanks to strict regulations, the 19th-century heritage of this quaint town 30 miles (48 km) northwest of Chicago has been preserved. The candy-filled Long Grove Confectionery store is a local institution. Annual events include the popular Chocolate Festival. ⬗ *Off Map • At Route 83 & Old Route 53 • Visitor Center: 1-847-634-0888 • Open Mon–Sat 10am–5pm, 11am–5pm Sun*

Brookfield Zoo

Over 5,900 animals live together in themed, naturalistic environments at this popular zoo. Zones include Tropic World, where thunderstorms occur regularly (you stay dry) and Habitat Africa, whose new Forest exhibit has shy okapi and a re-created African village. In Be A Bird House, see

Baha'i Temple

what kind of bird you'd be on a machine that measures your flapping ability. ⬗ *3300 Golf Rd, Brookfield • Map A5 • Metra station: Hollywood • Open 10am–5pm daily • 1-708-485-2200 • Adm. (2 and under, free) • DA*

Evanston

Just north of Chicago, this dynamic suburb brims with acclaimed restaurants, galleries, and independent shops. Northwestern University's Mary and Leigh Block Museum of Art and Sculpture Garden is well worth a visit, as is the historic Grosse Point Lighthouse and Maritime Museum. ⬗ *Map B2 • Visitors Bureau 1-847-328-1500 • El station: Davis*

AROUND TOWN

CHICAGO'S TOP 10

Left **Harold Washington Library Center** Right **Elevated train, The Loop**

The Loop

NAMED AFTER THE RING OF ELEVATED TRAIN TRACKS *that encircle it, this is downtown Chicago's core, and the city's financial and governmental hub. Abuzz with laptop-toting business folk during the week, the Loop is transformed on weekends when a veritable shopping frenzy erupts along its famous State Street. Those thirsty for culture also come flocking to view the area's many architecturally significant buildings and notable public art. A recent infusion of corporate dollars has given the Loop a real boost: the resulting restoration of old theaters and the promotion of the theater district has lured in more visitors, and the many great bars and restaurants that have sprung up mean that the area now offers a burgeoning nightlife.*

Lion, Art Institute of Chicago

🔟 Sights

1. Art Institute of Chicago
2. Sears Tower
3. Chicago Cultural Center
4. The El
5. Harold Washington Library Center
6. Chicago Board of Trade
7. State Street
8. State of Illinois Center
9. The Rookery
10. Millennium & Grant parks

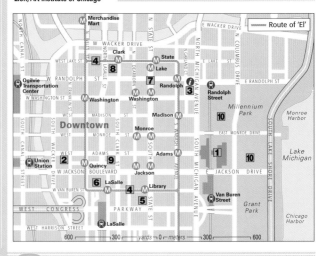

The Art Institute of Chicago

This extraordinary collection of exhibits spans over 4,000 years of international art, much of it donated by wealthy Chicago collectors (see pp8–11).

Sears Tower

An architectural superlative, the tower offers breathtaking bird's-eye views from its 103rd floor Skydeck, where you'll find yourself standing on top of 76,000 tons of steel (see pp12–13).

Chicago Cultural Center

Built in 1897 as the city's first main library, this magnificent Beaux Arts building was described at the time as the "people's palace." In 1991, the library moved out, allowing several galleries, performance spaces and a visitor information center to move in. Guided tours offer a historical overview of the building, which occupies an entire block and features one of the world's largest domes, designed by L. C. Tiffany, and rooms modeled after the Doge's Palace in Venice and the Acropolis in Athens. ◈ 78 E. Washington St. • Map L4 • 312-744-6630 • Open 8am–7pm Mon–Thu, 8am–6pm Fri, 9am–6pm Sat, 10am–6pm Sun • Tours 1:15pm Wed, Fri & Sat • Free • DA

The El

Originally called the Union Loop, this system of elevated trains came about after the 1871 Great Chicago Fire (see p34) when the city was rebuilt with such unexpected success that, within 20 years, its streets could no longer handle the influx of people, streetcars, and horses filling them. Today, four lines ring the business district – the

Tiffany Dome, Chicago Cultural Center

Orange, Purple, Pink, and Brown lines – with three others connecting it to destinations farther afield (see p56).

Harold Washington Library Center

Named after former city Mayor Harold Washington, Chicago's first Afro-American mayor (see p35), this is the largest public library building in the country. Its collections, which include a superlative Blues Archive and a vast children's library, fill an incredible 70 miles (110 km) of shelving. Architects Hammond, Beeby, and Babka incorporated architectural elements of several Chicago landmarks, such as The Rookery (see p70) and The Art Institute (see pp8–9) in the building's design: don't miss the ninth-floor Winter Garden atrium, which soars two stories to a spectacular glass dome. ◈ 400 S. State St. • Map K5 • Open 9am–7pm Mon–Thu, 9am–5pm Fri & Sat, 1–5pm Sun • Free • DA

Sears Tower

Around Town – The Loop

Borrow piano sheet music at the Harold Washington Library and tickle the ivories in one of the six free-to-use practice rooms.

69

Chicago Board of Trade

The Chicago Board of Trade (CBOT) was founded in 1848 to create a central marketplace in the fast-developing city, and moved to its current 45-story home in 1930. Designed by Holabird and Root, this landmark building is a stunning example of Art Deco. Capping the majestic limestone building is a huge statue of Ceres, the Roman goddess of grain and harvest. A glittering 23-story glass-and-steel addition designed by Helmut Jahn was completed in 1980. ❻ *141 W. Jackson Blvd. • Map K4 • Closed to the public until further notice*

State Street

This "great street" got its nickname from the 1922 hit song Chicago. Although it didn't always live up to this catchy moniker, it has won back many fans since its multi-million-dollar face-lift in 1996. It now sports replica Art Deco lampposts and subway entrances, and was listed on the National Register of Historic Places in 1998. This dynamic stretch has it all: shopping, history, education, architecture, theater, and dining. The atmosphere is especially merry during the run up to Christmas, when the Thanksgiving parade brings Santa to town, and department stores like Macy's *(see p74)* fill

Buckingham Fountain, Grant Park

The Loop's Sculpture

Setting a trend for public artwork Downtown, Pablo Picasso's untitled sculpture, simply known as "the Picasso," was donated to Chicago in 1967. The Loop's street corners now accommodate more than 100 sculptures, mosaics, and murals by both established and upcoming artists. A guide to the open-air artworks – the *Loop Sculpture Guide* – is available from the Chicago Cultural Center *(see p68).*

their windows with elaborate and imaginative decorations. ❼ *From Wacker Dr. to Congress Parkway • Map K4*

James R. Thompson Center

Also known as the State of Illinois Center, this striking 17-story, steel and granite structure shimmers with 24,600 curved glass panels. Helmut Jahn designed the controversial 1985 building to be a democratic fusion of government offices and public spaces, such as shops, restaurants, and art galleries. The soaring skylit atrium is sliced by internal glass elevator shafts and contains unusual, see-through escalators. Outside, the plaza features the intriguing 1984 sculpture *Monument with Standing Beast* by Jean Dubuffet. ❽ *100 W. Randolph St. • Map K4 • Atrium, shops, & food court open to public: 8:30am–6pm Mon–Fri • Free • DA*

The Rookery

This 11-story building, with its rusticated red granite base, was the country's largest office building and a precursor to modern skyscrapers when it was completed in 1888 by Burnham and Root *(see p37).* Its stunning skylit lobby was

State of Illinois Center

redesigned in 1907 by Frank Lloyd Wright *(see pp30–31)*, who added a grand staircase and hanging light fixtures, both of which carry his signature circle-in-square motif. The building's unusual name refers to the rooks that once roosted at the site. ⬡ *209 S. LaSalle St. • Map K4 • Open 9am–5pm Mon–Fri • Free • no DA*

Millennium & Grant parks

The modern Millennium Park *(see p62)* is Chicago's superb new adaptation of its "front yard". The park is home to a dynamic Frank Gehry-designed music pavilion and pedestrian bridge, and a vast sculpture by British artist Anish Kapoor. It also boasts lush gardens, restaurants, a winter ice rink, peristyle, and an interactive fountain by Spanish artist Jaume Plensa. The adjoining Grant Park *(see p62)* hosts many summer festivals including the Taste of Chicago *(see p50)*. It is also home to Museum Campus *(see p92)*, the Art Institute of Chicago *(see pp8–11)*, and the ornate 1927 Buckingham Fountain. ⬡ *Map L6 & L4 • Open daily • Free • DA*

A Day in The Loop

Morning

🕐 Start early with breakfast at the charming Atwood Café in the lobby of the historic **Hotel Burnham** *(see p116)*, with its beautifully reconstructed interior. Then stroll a block west to Daley Plaza to see the giant unnamed **Picasso sculpture**, stopping off at the Hot Tix booth at 78 W Randolph Street, to get half-price, same-day tickets to a Loop theater performance. Continue along Michigan Avenue, past the **Chicago Cultural Center** *(see p68)*, and south to **The Art Institute of Chicago**. A whirlwind tour of the highlights *(see pp10–11)*, all conveniently located on the upper level, can be done in a couple of hours, though you may want to come back for a second helping.

Afternoon

Either have lunch in The Art Institute's outdoor café or head west along **State Street** to eat at **Macy's** *(see p74)* legendary seventh-floor Walnut Room, a Chicago fixture since 1907. Then burn off the calories by shopping your way around the vast store and along the famous street that it's situated on. For pre-theater dining, try the sophisticated **Rhapsody** *(see p75)*, convenient for the **Symphony Center** *(see p48)* Or, on weekdays, try the all-you-can-eat buffet at **Trattoria No. 10** *(see p75)*.

Evening

After the show, hop a quick cab ride to stylish **Nine** *(see p75)* for a cocktail or some dancing late into the night in the slick second-floor Ghost Bar.

Around Town – The Loop

Left **Chicago Theater** Center **Fisher Building** Right **One North LaSalle**

TOP 10 Architectural Sites

Monadnock Building
At 16 stories, this Holabird and Roche designed building (1891) is one of the world's tallest all-masonry high-rises. Inside, there's a magnificent wrought-iron staircase *(see p36)*. ✆ *53 W. Jackson Blvd. • Map K4*

Marquette Building
Holabird and Roche also built this 1895 Chicago School structure with a steel skeleton and decorative ornamentation. ✆ *140 S. Dearborn St. • Map K4*

Reliance Building
Daniel H. Burnham's stunning glass-and-white-glazed-terra-cotta building (1895) is now the Hotel Burnham *(see p116)*.

Fisher Building
Another Chicago School edifice with a steel structure, this 1896 neo-Gothic building is also by Daniel H. Burnham. Aquatic motifs on the façade honor the building's first owner, L. G. Fisher. ✆ *343 S. Dearborn St. • Map K5*

Carson Pirie Scott Building
Eye-catching cast-iron swirls on part of the exterior of this building (1899 & 1903) express architect Louis H. Sullivan's love of elaborate detail.

Santa Fe Center
Daniel H. Burnham designed this elegant high-rise in 1904: its carved building signs are from Chicago's days as a railroad hub. The ground level houses the Chicago Architecture Foundation *(see p59)*.

Chicago Theater
The red marquee of this Beaux Arts-style theater is a symbol of Chicago. Built in 1921, today it is a performance venue. ✆ *175 N. State St. • Map K4*

One North LaSalle
This 1930-built, 49-story building was Chicago's tallest for 35 years, and is one of the city's best surviving examples of Art Deco architecture. ✆ *Map K4*

Inland Steel Building
One of the first skyscrapers to be built (in 1957) on steel, not concrete, pilings. It predated the John Hancock building *(see p12)* in using external supports. ✆ *30 W. Monroe St. • Map K4*

Federal Center
Flanked by Ludwig Mies van der Rohe's federal buildings, this plaza (1959–74) contains Alexander Calder's striking statue Flamingo (1974). ✆ *219 S. Dearborn St. • Map K4*

Around Town – The Loop

72

For more on Skyscrapers See p36–7

Left **Civic Opera Building** Center **Old St. Patrick's Church** Right **Palmer House Hilton**

🔟 Best of the Rest

Loop Theater District
A sidewalk plaque at Randolph and State Streets denotes Chicago's Theater District, a cluster of old and new theaters. ◎ *Map K4*

Civic Opera House
This 1929 structure was inspired by Paris's Opera Garnier. Inside, there are gleaming marble floors, crystal chandeliers, and a grand staircase *(see p48)*.

Symphony Center
At the heart of this center is Orchestra Hall (1904), the home of the Chicago Symphony Orchestra. A major 1997 extension added offices and the Rhapsody restaurant *(see p48)*.

Old St. Patrick's Church
Chicago's oldest church (1856) is crowned by two towers – one Romanesque, one Byzantine – symbolizing East and West. ◎ *700 W. Adams St. • Map J4*

Fine Arts Building
This historic landmark was designed by Solon S. Beman and completed in 1885. It was used as a carriage showroom by the Studebaker Company. ◎ *410 S. Michigan Ave. • Map L5*

Chicago Temple
A Gothic-inspired structure that was designed by Holabird and Roche in 1923. Under the majestic spire is a 35-seat chapel. ◎ *77 W. Washington St. • Map J4*

Federal Reserve Bank
This impressive structure is one of 12 regional Reserve banks. When it was first built in 1922, it had the largest bank vaults ever constructed. ◎ *230 S. LaSalle St. • Map K4*

Palmer House Hilton
The first Palmer House was destroyed in the Great Chicago Fire *(see p34)*. The current grand hotel is the third version and is lavishly decorated with frescos, Tiffany light fixtures, and marble floors *(see p116)*.

Daley Plaza
The location of the county court headquarters, Daley Plaza is best known for its giant steel unnamed Picasso sculpture (1967), donated by the artist. It was mocked when unveiled, but is now a city icon. ◎ *Map K4*

Four Seasons
Chagall's glittering 70-ft (21-m) long, rectangular slab (1974) is covered in thousands of tiles that depict the cycle of the seasons. ◎ *First National Plaza, at Dearborn and Monroe • Map K4*

Around Town – The Loop

73

Left **Artwork for sale in Gallery 37** Center **Clock at Macy's** Right **Poster Plus**

TOP 10 Shops

Macy's
1 Once Marshall Field's, Chicago's oldest and best-known department store continues to be famous for its elaborate Christmas displays, dazzling Tiffany dome, and iconic clock. Established nearly 100 years ago, it offers top styles for home and body *(see p58)*. Ⓢ *111 N. State St. • Map K2 • DA*

Filene's Basement
2 Here you'll find some fantastic budget-friendly buys and once-in-a-lifetime bargains on bridge, designer, and even couture goods. Ⓢ *1 N. State St. • Map K4 • DA*

Sears on State
3 After 18 years away, a hipper Sears returned to State Street in 2000 offering five levels of everything from tools to toddler outfits. Ⓢ *2 N. State St. • Map K2 • DA*

Prairie Avenue Bookshop
4 This wonderful bookstore is the world's largest that is dedicated to architecture and related fields. It's a staple for architecture students, but also a fascinating browse for anyone. Ⓢ *418 S. Wabash Ave. • Map K4 • Closed Sun • DA*

Jeweler's Center
5 On the strip commonly known as "Jeweler's Row" this one-stop-shop is a friendly place to source gold, pearls, watches, diamonds, and gems at relatively low prices. Ⓢ *5 S. Wabash Ave. • Map K4 • Closed Sun • DA*

Nordstrom Rack
6 High style on sale at a fraction of the original prices lure bargain hunters to this charming little sister of the upscale and pricey Nordstrom. Ⓢ *24 N. State St. • Map K4*

Poster Plus
7 This enormous store opposite The Art Institute of Chicago *(see pp8–11)* sells contemporary, vintage, and collectors' posters, as well as artsy gifts. Ⓢ *200 S. Michigan Ave. • Map L6 • DA*

Gallery 37 Store
8 Teenage artists involved in an arts training program create the incredible paintings, sculptures, and other artwork sold here. All proceeds from sales are returned to the program. Ⓢ *66 E. Randolph St. • Map L4 • DA*

Old Navy
9 This regional flagship store offers the ultimate Old Navy shopping experience, with two floors of discount jeans and T-shirts, and other casual comfort clothes at bargain prices. Ⓢ *35 N. State St. • Map K2 • DA*

Iwan Ries Tobacco
10 A smoker's paradise since 1897, this store now sells around 100 cigar brands, 15,000 pipes, and countless smoking accessories. It also contains a small tobacco museum. Ⓢ *19 S. Wabash Ave. • Map K2 • Closed Sun • DA*

Price Categories

Price categories include a three-course meal for one, a glass of house wine, tax, and a 15–20% tip.

$	under $20
$$	$20–$30
$$$	$30–$45
$$$$	$45–$60
$$$$$	over $60

Russian Tea Time

🔟 Places to Eat & Drink

1 Nine

This hip restaurant specializes in steaks and seafood. There's also a champagne bar and the Ghost Bar for drinks and dancing. ◎ *440 W. Randolph St. • Map J4 • 312-575-9900 • Closed Sat lunch & all day Sun • $$$$$*

2 Everest

The restaurant on the top floor of the Chicago Stock Exchange has dazzling views and to-die-for chocolate soufflé. ◎ *440 S. LaSalle St. • Map K5 • 312-663-8920 • Closed lunch, Sun & Mon • $$$$$*

3 Rhapsody

A perfect choice for modern American food (like the signature onion-crusted sturgeon) before or after a concert. ◎ *Symphony Center, 65 E. Adams St. • Map L4 • 312-786-9911 • Closed Sat lunch & Sun, except on concert days • $$$$*

4 Rivers

In the summer the deck of this elegant riverside restaurant offers some of the best views of the city. ◎ *30 S. Wacker Dr. • Map J4 • 312-559-1515 • Closed Sat lunch & Sun • $$$$*

5 Trattoria No. 10

Ravioli and risotto are the specialties here. A $12 buffet (plus $6 drink minimum) is available Monday through Friday evenings. ◎ *10 N. Dearborn St. • Map K3 • 312-984-1718 • Closed Sat lunch & Sun • $$$$*

6 Catch 35

This sophisticated seafood restaurant has live piano jazz in the evenings. Don't miss the key lime pie. ◎ *35 W. Wacker Dr. • Map K3 • 312-346-3500 • Closed Sat & Sun lunch • $$$$*

7 Ada's Famous Deli

Walk right in for generous portions of deli favorites such as matzo ball soup and stuffed cabbage. ◎ *14 S. Wabash Ave. • Map K4 • 312-214-4282 • $*

8 Atwood Café

Expect top-notch hotel dining, where creative American cuisine leans toward comfort food. ◎ *Hotel Burnham, 1 W. Washington St. • Map J4 • 312-368-1900 • $$$$*

9 Italian Village Restaurants

Choose between upscale Vivere, The Village with its extensive menu, or mid-priced La Cantina – all under one roof. ◎ *71 W. Monroe St. • Map K4 • 312-332-4040 (Vivere), 312-332-7005 (The Village & La Cantina) • Days closed vary • $$$–$$$$ • No DA*

10 Russian Tea Time

A spirited taste of Russia, where the vodka flows freely and the beef stroganoff is a crowd-pleaser. ◎ *77 E. Adams St. • Map L4 • 312-360-0000 • $$$$*

Left **Merchandise Mart** Center **Tiffany vases** Right **Carl Hammer Gallery, River North Gallery District**

Near North

HISTORY, CULTURE, AND COMMERCE *collide on Chicago's densely-packed Near North side. This area is a pleasure to explore on foot, whether motivated by a penchant for shopping or an appreciation of fine art and architecture. The city's toniest shopping boulevard – the Magnificent Mile, a.k.a. the Mag Mile – bridges the posh 19th-century mansions of the lakeside Gold Coast (which has its own clutch of upscale boutiques) and the former industrial warehouses of River North, now mostly converted into art galleries. In addition to these, two local art museums prove that "exhibitionism" in Chicago isn't just about the Art Institute (see pp10–11). But ultimately, it's the Magnificent Mile on a Saturday that says more about Midwestern vitality and giddy American consumerism than any other Chicago experience.*

Observation Deck, John Hancock Center

Sights

1. Magnificent Mile
2. John Hancock Center
3. Merchandise Mart
4. Museum of Contemporary Art
5. River North Gallery District
6. Gold Coast Area
7. Historic Water Tower & Pumping Station
8. Tribune Tower
9. Fourth Presbyterian Church
10. Hershey's Chicago

Previous Pages **James R. Thompson Center**

Magnificent Mile

1 Magnificent Mile
Whether you're a shopper or not, this store-lined strip warrants a visit if only to get a feel for the commercial pulse that seems to keep Chicago humming *(see pp26–7)*.

2 John Hancock Center
Skidmore, Owings & Merrill designed this 1970 landmark using the signature X's on the facade as cross-braces to help the 1,100-ft (335-m) building withstand the winds coming off Lake Michigan. An alternative to soaking up the view from the 94th-floor observatory is drinking it in from the Signature Room restaurant and lounge on the floors directly above. Many say you get a better view from here than from the South Side's Sears Tower – and the lines are usually shorter too. ◉ *875 N. Michigan Ave. • Map L2 • Observatory open 9am–11pm daily, Adm., DA • Signature Room open 11am–2:30pm Mon–Sat, 10am–2pm Sun, 5–10pm Sun–Thu, 5–11pm Fri & Sat, DA*

3 Merchandise Mart
This massive two-square-block edifice houses Chicago's premier interior design trade showrooms. When completed in 1930, the four million-sq-ft (390,000-sq-m) building was the largest in the world. Today, it is second only to the Pentagon in size, and is still the world's largest commercial building. A 90-minute guided tour includes a visit to several showrooms. ◉ *300 N. Wells St. • Map K3 • Free • DA • Tours 1pm Mon & Fri, call 312-527-7762, Adm. cash only*

4 Museum of Contemporary Art
One of the country's largest collections of international contemporary art, the MCA displays over 6,000 objects, from painting and sculpture to photography and video installations. Trendy Spago chef Wolfgang Puck runs the airy café, which draws both museum-goers and Mag Mile shoppers alike. In summer, the terraced sculpture garden enhances the MCA experience, while the front lawn often plays host to displays of performance art. ◉ *220 E. Chicago Ave. • Map L2 • Open Tue–Sun 10am–5pm (to 8pm Tue) • Adm. (free on Tue) • DA*

Sculpture, Museum of Contemporary Art

5 River North Gallery District
Said to be the most concentrated art hub in the US outside of Manhattan, this district is jammed with great galleries. Most are to be found in the handsome, 19th-century, converted brick warehouses found along either side of the El brown line. Huron and Superior Streets are particularly worth a visit. ◉ *Bounded by Merchandise Mart (south), Chicago Ave. (north), Orleans Ave. (west), Dearborn St. (east) • Map K3 • Chicago Gallery News 312-649-0064 • www.chicagogallerynews.com*

Stained glass, Fourth Presbyterian Church

Gold Coast Area
Chicago boasts many upscale neighborhoods, but none more historic and prestigious than the Gold Coast. Railroad, retail, and lumber tycoons built this elegant district in the decades following the Great Fire of 1871 (see p34), and its leafy streets are lined with 19th-century mansions interspersed with early 20th-century apartment buildings. There are no less than 300 designated historic landmarks in the Astor Street District alone, including buildings by Stanford White (such as 20 E. Burton Place), and Charnley House, designed by Louis Sullivan (assisted at the time by Frank Lloyd Wright). (1365 N. Astor Street). ✪ Map K1

Historic Water Tower & Pumping Station
When the Great Fire of 1871 swept north, only the 1869 Water Tower and Pumping Station escaped ruin. Built by William W. Botington, the castellated Gothic-Revival

Historic Water Tower

Water Tower, modeled after a medieval castle, was once called a "monstrosity" by critic Oscar Wilde. It now houses the City Gallery (specializing in photography), and the fountain and chairs outside make it a focal point for downtown street life. The Water Pumping station across the street still functions, and also houses a visitor center and the Lookingglass Theater, co-founded by Friends star David Schwimmer. ✪ Map K2 • Water Pumping Station & Tower 163 E. Pearson St., Visitor Center open 8am–7pm Mon–Thu, 8am–6pm Fri, 9am–6pm Sat, 10am–6pm Sun, 877-244-2246 • City Gallery open 10am–6:30pm Mon–Sat, 10am–5pm Sun, Free, 312-744-6630, DA

Tribune Tower
Topped by flying buttresses, this Gothic-style building was completed in 1925. Its faux historic design had won a competition organized by Colonel Robert McCormick, publisher of the Chicago Tribune, the newspaper whose offices still occupy the building. Look closely at the facade, which is embedded with over 120 stones collected by correspondents from famed sights. There's a rock hailing from each of the 50 states, as well as fragments from international monuments such as Greece's Parthenon, India's Taj Mahal, and The Great Wall of China. ✪ 435 N Michigan Ave • Map L3 • Tours by appointment

Fourth Presbyterian Church
The first Fourth Presbyterian church, dedicated in 1871, celebrated its first sermon just hours before it was incinerated in the Great Fire. Rebuilt in 1914 when

Magnificent Mile was the little-used Pine Street, today's church offers a peaceful respite from the now highly commercial boulevard. Designed by Ralph Adams Cram, one of the architects behind New York's Cathedral of St. John the Divine, it's not surprising that this church boasts a cathedral-like interior, with an impressive stained-glass west window. A tranquil courtyard is often the place for classical concerts in summer. ⓢ *126 E. Chestnut St. • Map K2 • Open 9am–6pm daily • Free • DA*

Hershey's Chicago
When candy-manufacturer Milton Hershey visited the city of Chicago in 1893, he purchased the equipment that he would use to revolutionize the chocolate industry. With mass production he was able to lower the cost of manufacturing milk chocolate, once a luxury item, making it affordable to all. Today, the Hershey Foods Corporation is the largest North American producer of chocolate and non-chocolate confectionary. Hershey's Chicago, a new themed store on Magnificent Mile, stocks all the well-known brands such as *Hershey's, Reese's,* and *Kit Kat,* as well as the latest products and goods unique to the Chicago store. Sugar-free versions of the most popular products are also available. A hit with children is the store's interactive "bake shoppe" where visitors can customize cookies, cupcakes, and brownies. ⓢ *822 N Michigan Ave • Map L2*

Store sign for Hershey's Chicago

A Day in the Near North

Morning
Line up early with the locals for a fortifying stack at The Original Pancake House (22 E. Bellevue Pl.). Afterward, stroll south on Rush Street to Oak Street. Take a left and walk the most exclusive shopping block in the city, where you can pop into stores such as Barneys New York. Once you hit Michigan Avenue, it's a short jaunt to the **John Hancock Center** *(see p79)* and its sky-high views. Back on terra firma, cross the street to the **Historic Water Tower** for a close-up look at a piece of Chicago's history. Lovers of modern art should cross Michigan again and head to the **Museum of Contemporary Art** *(see p79)* with its spacious galleries and sculpture garden.

Afternoon
Everyone will get what they want for lunch at Foodlife, a gourmet food court on the second level of the mall in **Water Tower Place** *(see p26).* You can shop the seven floors of Chicago's first ever vertical mall, and then shop some more – and sightsee – along the **Magnificent Mile** *(see pp26–7).* If you've worked up an appetite, stroll over to the **Drake Hotel** *(see p115)* for high tea, which serves until 5pm.

Evening
Alternatively, NoMI in the **Park Hyatt Chicago** *(see p115)* serves stylish contemporary fare (reservations needed), as befits the neighborhood. Or just join the smart set over cocktails at the Bar at the **Peninsula Chicago** *(see p115).*

Left **American Girl Place** Right **Paper Source**

TOP 10 Shopping

1 Ultimo
Oak Street's toniest designer boutique, Ultimo carries a range of cutting-edge European and American lines for women. ⊗ *114 E. Oak St. • Map L1*

2 Barneys New York
This branch of the Big Apple's downtown department store draws together the latest cosmetics, shoes, jewelry, accessories, and men's and women's apparel in a minimalist, open-plan, tri-level space. ⊗ *25 E. Oak St. • Map L1*

3 Bloomingdale's
An outpost of New York's hometown department store that features in-store designer boutiques and a well-stocked shoe department. ⊗ *900 N. Michigan Ave. • Map L2*

4 Ikram
Launched by a former Ultimo buyer, Ikram specializes in high-end women's fashion sold at top dollar. Chic wares and lines change seasonally, but shop assistance is uniformly personal. ⊗ *873 N. Rush St. • Map L2*

5 Polo/Ralph Lauren
This massive four-story shop so thoroughly transforms itself from a store to a swell den devoted to Lauren's to-the-manor-born lifestyle – note the horse and hound paintings throughout – that it warrants a visit from even the less well-heeled among us. ⊗ *750 N. Michigan Ave. • Map L2*

6 American Girl Place
Parents accompanying girls age four to 12 make a beeline to this store, the only retail outlet of the popular American Girl line of dolls. A theater and café *(see p57)* supplement three floors devoted to dolls, books, and accessories. ⊗ *111 E. Chicago Ave. • 312-943-9400 • Map L2*

7 Anthropologie
Women's apparel with a bohemian bent and housewares gathered from around the world sell briskly at this loft-like store. ⊗ *1120 N. State St. • Map K2*

8 P.O.S.H.
Recalling the days of elegant steamships and grand hotels, this store uses old-fashioned suitcases and steamer trunks to lovingly display vintage china and silverware engraved with hotel and ship logos. ⊗ *613 N. State St. • Map K2*

9 Paper Source
This arty River North shop is part art supply store, part stationer. The creative selection of cards and small gifts includes handmade stationery, cloth-covered sketchbooks, and novel desktop accessories. ⊗ *232 W. Chicago Ave. • Map J2*

10 Fly By Nite Gallery
Amid the River North fine art galleries, Fly By Nite sells Art Nouveau and Art Deco decorative arts, including malachite jewelry, art-glass lamps and vases, and collectible pottery. ⊗ *714 N. Wells St. • Map K2*

Most Near North shops are open 10am–7pm Mon–Sat & 11am–6pm Sun and have DA.

Price Categories

Price categories include a three-course meal for one, a glass of house wine, tax, and a 15–20% tip.

$	under $20
$$	$20–$30
$$$	$30–$45
$$$$	$45–$60
$$$$$	over $60

Frontera Grill

🔟 Places to Eat & Drink

1 Frontera Grill
Chef Rick Bayless' regional Mexican cuisine warrants the two-margarita waits that inevitably face diners here. ⓢ 445 N. Clark St. • Map K2 • 312-661-1434 • Closed Sun & Mon • Reservations only for groups of 5+ • $$$

2 Keefer's
A steakhouse that goes beyond the men's club stereotype, also serving French specials and ample fish selections. ⓢ 20 W. Kinzie St. • Map K3 • 312-467-9525 • Closed Sun & lunch Sat • $$$$$

3 Bin 36
A wine bar of warehouse proportions, Bin 36 engenders an infectious enthusiasm for wine and food. The many small dishes encourage sampling. ⓢ 333 N. Dearborn St. • Map K3 • 312-755-9463 • $$$

4 RL
An in-store steakhouse and power-eatery, furnished in upper crust style by the Ralph Lauren Home shop while elegantly attired hostesses sport Polo. ⓢ 115 E. Chicago Ave. • Map L2 • 312-475-1100 • $$$$

5 Pierrot Gourmet
Run by the elegant Peninsula hotel, this café serves inventive salads, open sandwiches and pastries. ⓢ 108 E. Superior St. • Map L2 • 312-573-6749 • No reservations • $$

6 Coco Pazzo
In the gallery district Coco Pazzo prepares dramatic, earthy Italian cuisine in an impressive loft space. ⓢ 300 W. Hubbard St. • Map K3 • 312-836-0900 • Closed Sat & Sun lunch • $$$$$

7 Kevin
Chef Kevin Shikami has struck out alone, offering a daily-changing menu that puts an Asian spin on French cuisine. Enjoy a tuna tartare and favorite cocktail at the wood and slate bar. ⓢ 9 W. Hubbard St. • Map L3 • 312-595-0055 • Closed Sun • $$$$$

8 Pump Room
A jazz trio, opulent decor, and a forward-leaning continental menu serve diners here. Celebrities love its famed "booth 1." ⓢ 1301 N. State Pkwy. • Map K1 • 312-266-0360 • $$$$

9 Whiskey Bar & Grill
Run by Rande Gerber, husband of supermodel Cindy Crawford, this sophisticated, sleek bar attracts a trendy crowd. ⓢ 1015 N. Rush St. • Map L2 • 312-475-0300

10 Zebra Lounge
A classic piano lounge, the Zebra is intimate, friendly, and decorated wall to wall in animal prints. It's a funky place to drink cocktails in the Gold Coast. ⓢ 1220 N. State St. • Map K2 • 312-642-5140

Unless otherwise stated, all restaurants recommend reservations, accept credit cards, have DA, and are open for lunch and dinner.

Left **Armitage/Halsted Shopping District** Right **Butterfly, Peggy Notebaert Nature Museum**

Northside

ENCOMPASSING PARTS OF OLD TOWN, *Lincoln Park, Lakeview, and Wrigleyville,* Chicago's Northside boasts upscale restaurants and chi-chi boutiques galore, as well as some of the city's best bars and one of its most progressive theater companies, the Steppenwolf (see p48). Older buildings have been transformed into beautiful condominiums, while stylish new apartments are springing up on empty lots. In season, nearby Wrigley Field fans bolster the lively Wrigleyville atmosphere by swarming the surrounding streets and bars – whether or not the Cubs win. The vibrant gay hub of "Boys Town" is also in this area, while running along Northside's eastern border is the incredible lakefront, with sand volleyball and a beach bar heating up as soon as the temperature allows.

Tiger, Lincoln Park Zoo

Around Town – Northside

🔟 Sights

1. Lincoln Park Zoo
2. Wrigley Field
3. Peggy Notebaert Nature Museum
4. Boys Town
5. Armitage/Halsted Shopping District
6. Chicago Historical Society
7. Lincoln Park Conservatory
8. North Avenue Beach
9. Elks National Memorial Building
10. Francis Dewes Mansion

Lincoln Park Zoo
Who's watching who at this beloved city zoo, which attracts more than three million visitors annually (see pp24–5).

Wrigley Field
Built in 1914, this is the USA's oldest National League baseball park. Home team, the Chicago Cubs, haven't won a World Series championship since 1908 (before the field even existed), but that doesn't stop Northsiders from being behind them every step of the way. In season (March–September), spending an afternoon cheering on the "Cubbies" in this marvelous stadium, with its ivy-clad walls, is a quintessential Chicago experience.
◈ 1060 W. Addison St. • Map D1 • 1-773-404-2827 • Box Office open 8am–6pm Mon–Fri, 9am–4pm Sat & Sun • Adm. • DA

Peggy Notebaert Nature Museum
This museum's sloping, beige exterior was inspired by the sand dunes that once occupied its site. Inside are a host of engrossing interactive exhibits, the highlight being the walk-through Butterfly Haven, a light-filled space, constantly aflutter. The outdoor grounds, with their native wild-

Wrigley Field

Boys Town

flowers and prairie grasses, are perfect for a peaceful walk or rest.
◈ 2430 N. Cannon Dr. • Map F3 • 773-755-5100 • Open 9am–4:30pm Mon–Fri, 10am–5pm Sat & Sun • Adm. • DA

Boys Town
Strolling down North Halsted Street, it's fairly evident you're in Chicago's gay neighborhood when you hit shops called Gay Mart, Cupid's Treasures, and a club named Manhole. Just 30 years ago, this area – officially East Lakeview – was pretty shabby, the bars were without signs, and parking was a cinch. But now buzzing Boys Town is gay central – by day and by night.
◈ N. Halsted St. (& much of Broadway) from Belmont Ave.–Grace St., & Clark St. from Belmont–Addison Aves. • Map E1–2

Armitage/Halsted Shopping District
This area of unique boutiques is a boon for fashionistas. Dozens of shops here sell everything from sophisticated evening wear to high-end accessories. Many of the stores occupy renovated Victorian town homes, set along pretty, tree-lined streets.
◈ Armitage Ave. from Halsted St.–Racine Ave., & Halsted St. from Webster–Armitage Aves. • Map E4

For more Chicago shopping See pp58–9

Lincoln Park Conservatory

Chicago History Museum

Focusing on Illinois and Chicago history since settler days, this museum was established in 1856 and is the city's oldest cultural institution. One of the society's first donors bequeathed his collection of Lincoln memorabilia: the ex-president's deathbed is one of the items displayed. Visitors can climb aboard the Pioneer locomotive, while events such as the World's Columbian Exposition and the Great Chicago Fire *(see p34)*, are brought to life by photographs, decorative arts, and other exhibits. There are also costumes belonging to famous figures, from George Washington to sportsman Michael Jordan. ⊛ *1601 N. Clark St.* • *Map K2* • *Open 9:30am–4:30pm Mon–Sat (8pm Thu), 12–5pm Sun* • *Adm. (free Mon)* • *DA*

Lincoln Park Conservatory

Take a free trip to the tropics at this spacious conservatory, just next to Lincoln Park Zoo. Opened in 1893, the glass structure is a year-round, 80° F (40° C) sanctuary from the Chicago's bustle, and offers a welcome respite from the city's long winters. Paths meander past lush palms, flourishing ferns, and exquisite 100-year-old orchids. Avoid the crowds by coming on a weekday when, unless a seasonal show is taking place, it's a quiet space, with the sound of trickling water as background music. ⊛ *2400 N. Stockton Dr.* • *Map F3* • *Open 9am–5pm daily* • *Free* • *DA*

North Avenue Beach

When summer finally graces Chicago with its presence, locals of all ages and nationalities converge on this short, but inviting stretch of beach. Running along its edge is the lakefront path, where cyclists, in-line skaters, runners, and walkers stream by. An outdoor gym gives confident folks a place to strut their stuff, sand volleyball courts allow the energetic to let off steam, and the rooftop bar of the steamship-shaped beach house is perfect for downing a cool drink while lazily watching the activity below. ⊛ *Lakeshore Dr. & North Ave.* • *Map F4* • *Open dawn to dusk* • *Lifeguards on duty from Memorial Day–Labor Day.*

Chicago Historical Society

For more on Chicago parks and beaches See pp 62–3

9 Elks National Memorial Building

The Benevolent and Protective Order of Elks, an American fraternity (founded in 1868 and still going strong), built this magnificent structure in 1926 to honor its World War I veterans. It's since been re-dedicated to pay homage to World War II, Korean and Vietnam war veterans. Two larger-than-life elk statues flank the wide entrance steps, while inside, every inch is richly decorated. The 100-ft (30-m) marble rotunda, murals depicting the Sermon on the Mount, intricate windows, and allegorical bronze sculptures are awe-inspiring. ✪ *2750 N. Lakeview Ave. • Map E2 • Open 9am–5pm Mon–Fri; mid-Apr–mid-Nov also open 10am–5pm Sat & Sun • Free • DA*

10 Francis Dewes Mansion

Nostalgic German immigrant Francis Dewes, a self-made millionaire, commissioned this elaborate home in 1896. Built in the eclectic Gründerzeit style – a German counterpart to Beaux Arts – its entrance steps, stone statues, and ornate carved curlicues certainly stand out from the neat rows of adjacent brick apartment buildings. Interior highlights include mosaic floors, a fountain, and wrought-iron chandeliers. ✪ *503 W. Wrightwood Ave. • Map E3 • 773-865-6819 • Tours by appointment only*

Francis Dewes Mansion

Exploring Northside

Morning

🕐 Fuel up for the day at one of Lincoln Park's favorite breakfast joints, **Frances'** (2552 N. Clark St.), where they serve a wonderfully fluffy French toast. Afterwards, stroll east down Wrightwood Avenue, and you'll pass the ornate **Francis Dewes Mansion**. Keep walking until you come to the **Lincoln Park Zoo** *(see pp24–5)*, where you can take a ride on the wild side on the African Safari motion simulator, complete with 3D visuals. Then see all the animals in person, before breaking for lunch with a view at **Café Brauer**, built in 1908 by Prairie School architect Dwight Perkins.

Afternoon

During warm weather, head to the lakefront along Fullerton Avenue where you can stroll, rent bikes, sunbathe, or even brave the ever-chilly Lake Michigan waters. In colder months, catch a bus (nos. 22 or 151) and immerse yourself in the exhibits at the **Chicago Historical Society**, or take a five-minute cab ride to **Armitage/Halsted Shopping District** *(see p85)* for some classy retail therapy.

Evening

This part of town has an abundance of good eateries: hop the El four stops or cab it to try **Mia Francesca's** *(see p41)*, a lively Italian trattoria where the pasta dishes are big enough for two, and there's an excellent wine list. Still going strong? Round off your day with a visit to **Kingston Mines** *(see p46)* – just a short cab-ride away – to hear some of best blues that the city has to offer.

Left **Barker & Meowsky** Right **Cynthia Rowley**

TOP 10 Shops

1 Isabella Fine Lingerie
This charming boutique has something silky, soft, and sexy for women whose sizes range from barely there to 44JJ. You'll also find teddies, bustiers, pajamas, and nightgowns.
⊛ 1101 W. Webster St. • Map E3

2 Cynthia Rowley
Internationally acclaimed clothing designer Cynthia Rowley grew up in Chicago, so it's fitting that one of her upscale boutiques is here. Her collection of dresses, accessories, and separates is trendy and feminine.
⊛ 808 W. Armitage Ave. • Map E4

3 Lori's Designer Shoes
Devoted shoe hounds flock to this Lincoln Park store for its hot styles at discounted prices. The floors and walls are stacked high with boxes for handy self-serve try-on access. ⊛ 824 W. Armitage Ave. • Map E4

4 Beatnix
This store boasts the best supply of costumes and vintage gear in the city, including wigs, distinctive mod jewelry, and make-up, as well as day-to-day items. ⊛ 3400 N. Halsted St. • Map E2

5 Unabridged Bookstore
Known for its large gay and lesbian section, this Boys Town (see p85) bookstore also stocks books of all types, particularly kids' and Spanish language books. ⊛ 3521 N. Broadway. • Map E2

6 Hubba-Hubba
Women appreciate this boutique for its romantic and flirty vintage fashions and jewelry. It also sells new items with a retro feel. ⊛ 3309 N. Clark St. • Map F4

7 The Leigh Gallery
Set in the heart of Lakeview, this gallery provides an inviting setting for art suited to all tastes, from modern to old-school classic, watercolor to sculpture.
⊛ 3306 N. Halsted St. • Map E2

8 Barker & Meowsky
Four-legged friends are the focus at this store. From ceramic dog bowls to catnip-filled toys, rhinestone-studded collars to cookie-shaped dog biscuits, this store is a pet's best friend.
⊛ 1003 W. Armitage Ave. • Map E4

9 Uncle Fun
This toy store is especially fun for grownups who yearn to feel like a kid. You'll find retro items like Mr. T coloring books, silly accessories like oversized sunglasses, and gag gifts like the tried-and-true whoopie cushion.
⊛ 1338 W. Belmont Ave. • Map E2

10 American Apparel
Simple, functional, and wildly popular, this manufacturer and retailer of clothing for men, women, kids, and dogs, which hails from Los Angeles, lays particular emphasis on well-made basics in bright colors and at reasonable prices. ⊛ 3126 N. Broadway • Map E2

Left **Kit Kat Lounge** Right **Bucks Saloon**

🔟 Gay & Lesbian Bars & Clubs

1 Circuit/Rehab
At Circuit, men often dance shirtless to grinding house music. In contrast, the Rehab lounge bar is a sophisticated chill-out spot. ◈ 3641 N. Halsted St. • Map E2 • Circuit: open Thu–Sun, Adm.

2 The Closet
This dance club attracts a mostly lesbian crowd, but gay men and straight couples also groove to R&B, rap, dance, and diva videos. ◈ 3325 N. Broadway • Map E2

3 Roscoe's Tavern
A young, preppy set packs this neighborhood bar for its antique décor, cozy fireplace, poppy dance tunes, pool table, and, in summer, backyard beer garden. ◈ 3356 N. Halsted St. • Map E2

4 Sidetrack
Find some of the best cruising at this vast, four-room bar with more than two dozen video monitors that highlight a different theme (like show tunes or 1980s music) every night. ◈ 3349 N. Halsted St. • Map E2

5 Spin
One of Boys Town's most diverse clubs: gay, lesbian, bi, and straight crowds mingle at this dance club and lounge. ◈ 800 W. Belmont Ave. • Map E2

6 Kit Kat Lounge & Supper Club
Martinis come in 52 flavors at this swanky spot, where female impersonators divert attention from significant others with their lip-synching talent. ◈ 3700 N. Halsted St. • Map E2 • Closed Mon

7 Berlin
For 20 years, this edgy club has attracted every type from straight girls to drag queens. After midnight, the dance floor hits its peak, rocking with a stellar sound system and light show. ◈ 954 W. Belmont Ave. • Map E2

8 Cocktail
This laid-back club is ideal for sipping must-try martinis, while Boys Town people-watching through wall-to-wall windows. ◈ 3359 N. Halsted St. • Map E2

9 Gentry on Halsted
Piano players and singers perform nightly for appreciative and participative audiences at this cabaret club. ◈ 3320 N. Halsted St. • Map E2

10 Bucks Saloon
A friendly, local bar (for boys and girls) where deer, elk, moose, and buck heads adorn the walls. The outdoor beer garden is wild in summer. ◈ 3439 N. Halsted St. • Map E2

Left **Guthrie's Tavern** Right **Decorative Brickwork at Schubas Tavern & Harmony Grill**

Neighborhood Bars

1 Schubas Tavern & Harmony Grill
Twenty-somethings dress down for beer, live music, and a great restaurant that packs in crowds, especially on the patio during warm-weather weekends. ✎ *3159 N. Southport Ave. • Map D1*

2 Four Farthings Tavern
This casual, family-owned bar is a perfect spot to kick back with one of 18 beers on tap, a single-malt whisky, or a glass of wine. ✎ *2060 N. Cleveland Ave. • Map E3*

3 Bar Louie on the Park
With the chain's signature wrap-around bar and bright mosaics, this bar is a comfortable favorite for young professionals who appreciate the moderately priced drinks, plenty of tap beers, and huge sandwiches. ✎ *1800 N. Lincoln Ave. • Map E3*

4 The Duke of Perth
This Scottish pub hits the mark, with nearly 90 varieties of single-malt whisky and plenty of Celtic paraphernalia and music. ✎ *2913 N. Clark St. • Map F4*

5 Guthrie's Tavern
Amid chitchat and free pretzels, boisterous patrons play board games. Come early for the best choice. ✎ *1300 W. Addison St. • Map D1*

6 John Barleycorn Memorial Pub
Disguised as a laundry during Prohibition, this cozy pub has been dispensing beer and spirits for over a hundred years. ✎ *658 W. Belden Ave. • Map E3*

7 Red Lion Pub
British ex-pats hang here for a taste of home that fits the bill with plenty of pints from across the pond. Upstairs is an outdoor deck for warm-weather carousing. ✎ *2446 N. Lincoln Ave. • Map E3*

8 Southport Lanes & Billiards
During the day, this is a laid-back bar: at night, a rowdy young crowd covets turns at the four hand-set bowling lanes. ✎ *3325 N. Southport Ave. • Map D1*

9 Wrightwood Tap
The centrally positioned bar, promotes an open, *Cheers*-type feel, with conversation flowing among patrons. TVs typically air college sports, while dart boards provide participatory entertainment. ✎ *1059 W. Wrightwood Ave. • Map E3*

10 The Tin Lizzie
A sports bar-and-dance club, Tin Lizzie is wall-to-wall with twenty- to thirtysomethings most weekend nights, when DJs spin a variety of tunes. ✎ *2483 N. Clark St. • Map F4*

Unless otherwise stated, all bars and clubs are open daily and have DA. At weekends many stay open until 2/3am.

North Pond

ᴛᴏᴘ10 Restaurants

1 North Pond
This pond-side restaurant (a former skaters "warming house") serves up American gourmet cuisine. ◈ 2610 N. Cannon Dr. • Map F3 • 1-773-477-5845 • Closed Mon, lunch (except Jun, Jul, Aug, Sep, & Sun) • $$$$

2 Ambria
Tuxedoed staff set an elegant tone at this French special-occasion favorite. ◈ 2300 N. Lincoln Park West • Map F3 • 1-773-472-5959 • Closed lunch, Sun • $$$$$

3 Charlie Trotter's
Light French food is artfully designed by master chef Charlie Trotter at this internationally acclaimed restaurant. ◈ 816 W. Armitage Ave. • Map E4 • 1-773-248-6228 • Closed Mon & Sun, lunch • $$$$$

4 Geja's Café
The ultimate fondue in a romantic setting. Choose cheese or hot oil, or just opt for the divine chocolate dessert fondue. ◈ 340 W. Armitage Ave. • Map E4 • 1-773-281-9101 • Closed lunch • No DA • $$$

5 erwin
Chef Erwin Drechsler offers up a "melting-pot" cuisine, complemented by a superb wine list. Sunday brunch is a real treat. ◈ 2925 N. Halsted St. • Map E2 • 1-773-528-7200 • Closed Mon, lunch (except Sun) • $$

6 Tarasacas
Mexican food gets a fancy touch at this colorful restaurant. Nights get spirited as diners down huge margaritas. ◈ 2585 N. Clark St. • Map F4 • 1-773- 549-2595 • Closed lunch (except Sat & Sun) • $$

7 Robinson's No. 1 Ribs
The perfect, low-key spot for getting messy with thick, saucy barbecue ribs. A back patio opens during warm weather. ◈ 655 W. Armitage Ave. • Map E4 • 312-337-1399 • Closed Mon, Sat lunch • No DA • $$

8 Stanley's Kitchen & Tap
Comfort food, like macaroni cheese and apple pie, is the draw at this family-friendly spot. The all-you-can-eat brunch gets packed. ◈ 1970 N. Lincoln Ave. • Map E3 • 312-642-0007 • Closed Mon lunch • $$

9 Ann Sather
Known for its scrumptious breakfasts, this Swedish restaurant also serves lunch and dinner specialties such as meatballs. ◈ 929 W. Belmont Ave. • Map E2 • 1-773-348-2378 • $

10 Mia Francesca
The wait for the generous portions of flavorful pastas, seafood, and chicken at this lively eatery is definitely worth it. ◈ 3311 N. Clark St. • Map F4 • 1-773-281-3310 • Closed lunch • $$$

Unless otherwise stated, all restaurants recommend reservations, accept credit cards, have DA, and are open for lunch and dinner.

91

Left **Adler Planetarium** Right **Shedd Aquarium (left) & Field Museum (right), Museum Campus**

South Loop

JUST SOUTH OF THE *business-centric Loop, this sprawling area mixes ethnic enclaves such as Chinatown (founded in the 1870s by migrant transcontinental railroad workers) with uppercrust addresses, built after the Great Chicago Fire of 1871 (see p34). The region has many Chicago "must-sees," but the jewel in the crown is undisputedly the impressive Museum Campus: here, the Field Museum, John G. Shedd Aquarium, and Adler Planetarium celebrate the wonders of the earth, sea, and sky respectively, collectively drawing over four million visitors each year. The highway that once separated the Field from its neighbors has been replaced by an inviting green campus, where cyclists and skaters join museum-goers on the plant-bordered paths in fair weather.*

 Sights

1 Field Museum
2 John G. Shedd Aquarium
3 Adler Planetarium
4 Prairie Avenue District
5 Blues Heaven Foundation
6 Maxwell Street Market
7 Museum of Contemporary Photography
8 Chinatown
9 National Vietnam Veterans Art Museum
10 Jane Addams' Hull House

Seals, Shedd Aquarium

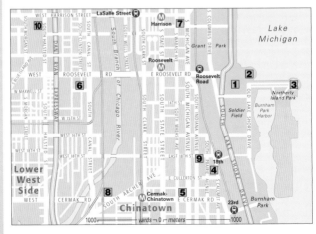

Field Museum
One of the three lakefront institutions to occupy the 57-acre (23-ha) Museum Campus, this vast museum boasts a collection of more than 20 million fascinating natural history and anthropological artifacts *(see pp14–15)*.

John G. Shedd Aquarium
The second of the three Museum Campus sights, the Shedd is also one of the oldest public aquariums in the world. Dive in to discover the many treasures of the aquatic world *(see pp22–3)*.

Blues Heaven Foundation

Adler Planetarium
This, the first planetarium in the Western Hemisphere, completes the Museum Campus trio. Visit its numerous galleries to walk among the stars, explore the worlds that orbit the Sun, and be enlightened by 1,000 years of astronomical discovery. Don't miss the opportunity to catch the Sky Theater show, which is projected on the 68-ft (21-m) dome of the historic Zeiss planetarium. The virtual reality events in the StarRider Theater are also awe-inspiring, launching you into the outer reaches of space and even give you the chance to interact with the show via a panel in the armrest. ® *1300 S. Lake Shore Dr. • Map M6 • Open summer (Jun–Sep) 9:30am–6pm daily; winter 9:30am–4:30pm daily; first Fri each month 9:30am–10pm; for showtimes call 312-922-7827 • Adm. • DA*

Figurine, Field Museum

Prairie Avenue District
Of the wealthy enclaves both north and south of the Chicago River that grew up following the Great Fire of 1871, Prairie Avenue was the most fashionable – and Chicago's ritziest. Only a few of its mansions remain today, of which two are open to the public (by tour only): the imposing, Romanesque-Revival 1887 Glessner House, and Chicago's oldest remaining building – Clarke House – built in 1836 in the Greek-Revival style by New York emigré Henry B. Clarke.
® *Map C5 • For info on walking-tours (Jul–Sep, on alternating weekends) call 312-326-1480 • Clarke House, 1827 S. Indiana Ave., tours noon, 1 & 2pm Wed–Sun, adm., DA • Glessner House, 1800 S. Prairie Ave., tours 1, 2 & 3pm Wed–Sun, adm., no DA*

Blues Heaven Foundation
Located in the former studios of Chess Records, where blues greats from Muddy Waters to Willie Dixon once recorded, Blues Heaven has an interesting collection of records, photos, and stage costumes dedicated to Chicago's blues style and its performers. Chess music plays on the PA, and there are occasional live performances. Rock aficionados will note the address is the namesake of a Rolling Stones song. ® *2120 S. Michigan Ave. • Map C5 • For tours call 312-808-1286 • Closed Sun • Adm. • Limited DA*

Feel like playing the blues? At Blues Heaven Foundation, staff say they can teach visitors the harmonica in 10 minutes.

93

Fresh produce, Maxwell Street Market

6 Maxwell Street Market
Both 19th-century European immigrants and 20th-century African-American settlers fleeing the Deep South got their entrepreneurial start selling from pushcarts around Maxwell Street. In 1994 the market was relocated to make way for the new University of Illinois at Chicago and, while a shadow of its former self, it still makes for a vibrant Sunday morning. Don't expect valuable finds; do expect plenty of Mexican housewares and used tools. But the occasional treasure, such as a vintage fur coat, does show up.

Architectural detail, Chinatown

Perhaps the best reason to visit is to try the homemade tacos from the Mexican food stalls that line the street. ◈ 548 W. Roosevelt Rd. • Map J6 • Open 7am–3pm Sun • Free

7 Museum of Contemporary Photography
Run by and located in Columbia College Chicago, this museum is one of a kind in the Midwest. It exhibits the portfolios of international modern masters, with shows (including student shows) tending toward the experimental rather than the traditional documentary. Changing exhibitions also present a healthy mixture of local talents and well-established ones, such as Gary Winogrand and William Eggleston. Frequent gallery talks give curators and artists the chance to discuss the shows with museum-goers. ◈ 600 S. Michigan Ave. • Map L5 • Open 10am–5pm, Mon–Fri (to 8pm Thu), noon–5pm Sat • Free • DA

8 Chinatown
Crowned by the landmark Chinatown Gate spanning Wentworth Avenue, Chicago's Chinatown isn't that large – running roughly eight blocks – but it is colorful. Home to Chicago's oldest Asian community, Chinatown was founded in the 19th century by transcontinental railroad workers fleeing West Coast prejudice. It continues to be a place where Cantonese and Mandarin are spoken far more widely than English. Stroll Wentworth to see the ornate On Leong Tong Building, buy fresh almond cookies from Chinese bakeries, peruse the many import and herbal shops, or chow down in one of the dozens of local restaurants. ◈ Around Wentworth Ave. & Cermak Rd. • Map B5

9 National Vietnam Veterans Art Museum
A moving tribute to the horrors of war, this museum, started in the late 1970s, now showcases over 1,000 works by more than 130 artists once involved in the conflict. Most of the artworks, which include paintings, sculptures, and drawings, as well as prose and poetry, come from former US soldiers, doctors and

R. R. Yonkha's *This Is How You Died,*
National Vietnam Veterans Art Museum

POWs, though powerful entries
by former Viet Cong and native
Cambodians attest to the universal
effects of the conflict.
⊗ *1801 S. Indiana Ave. • Map C5*
• 312-326-0270 • Open 11am–6pm Tue–Fri,
10am–5pm Sat • Adm. • DA

10 Jane Addams' Hull House
When European immigrants
were flooding Chicago to work
in its rail and stock yards during
the late 19th and early 20th
centuries, Jane Addams bought
Hull House for a specific
purpose. From here, she offered
social services and facilities to
this immigrant working class,
including day care, employment
counselling and art classes. A
great social reformer and winner
of the 1931 Nobel Peace Prize,
Addams also championed the
rights of women and helped
usher in child labor laws. Her
original office, furnishings, and
artwork are still in place for
visitors to see, supplemented
by temporary exhibits that tell
the story of the settlement at
Hull House and the invaluable
work of its residents. ⊗ *800 S.
Halsted St. • Map H5 • Open 10am–4pm
Tue–Fri, noon–4pm Sun • Free • DA*

Exploring South Loop

Morning

🕐 Start by grabbing coffee
and an oreo cookie
flapjack at **The Bongo
Room** (1152 S. Wabash
Ave., 312-291-0100). From
there, walk through Grant
Park to Museum Campus.
Here you can choose
between the **Field
Museum** *(see pp14–15)*,
Adler Planetarium
(see p93), and **Shedd
Aquarium** *(see pp22–3)*
all within walking distance
of each other. If you plan
to visit other museums on
your trip, it makes sense
to purchase a City Pass
(see p108). If you opt to
see the highlights of each,
end up at the Shedd, where
the **Soundings** restaurant
offers good food and great
views overlooking the lake.

Afternoon

Hail a cab (plenty wait outside the museums) or
walk to the nearby pedes-
trian bridge at 18th Street
to get to the **Prairie
Avenue District** *(see p93)*,
where you can stroll the
historic streets and maybe
even catch the 3pm tour
of the **Glessner House**
(see p93). If you've still
got the energy, walk one
block west to the fasci-
nating **National Vietnam
Veterans Art Museum**.

Evening

Head over to Wabash
Avenue for an early supper
at one of the trendy
eateries on what is now
a burgeoning strip. Mayor
Richard Daley has been
known to frequent **Gioco**
(see p97) for its stellar
Italian fare (reservations
are recommended).
Ready for more? Then
stay up late to hear the
blues at **Buddy Guy's
Legends** *(see p96)*.

Left **Diners, Hawkeye's Bar & Grill** Right **Bar Louie Taylor**

Bars & Clubs

Buddy Guy's Legends
Run by bluesman Buddy Guy, this club is arguably the city's best. To get a table, come early and dine on decent barbecue.
⊛ 754 S. Wabash Ave. • Map L5

Hothouse
Not-for-profit Hothouse serves up a gumbo of music in art-filled digs. Acts range from jazz to Afro-pop, with a smattering of poetry readings and performance art.
⊛ 31 E. Balbo Dr. • Map L5

M Lounge
Listen to traditional and modern jazz in style on comfy couches and low-slung seating in cranberry, chocolate, and sage. Stop by for live jazz on Wednesdays.
⊛ 1520 S. Wabash Ave. • Map K6

The Velvet Lounge
Ignore the threadbare decor; The Velvet Lounge offers some of the city's best jazz including jam sessions with the bar's owner, a saxman himself. ⊛ 67 E. Cermak Rd.
• Map B5 • Cash only • Closed Mon

NetWorks
A popular gathering place, NetWorks airs news and sports on an array of TVs. ⊛ Hyatt Regency McCormick Place, 2233 S. Martin Luther King Dr. • Map D5 • Free

South Loop Club
This sports bar boasts a 70-inch TV screen, 10 different draft beers, and twice as many bottles, plus a full menu. ⊛ 701 S. State St. • Map K5

Bar Louie Taylor
One of several popular Bar Louies in town, this Little Italy outpost plies generous martinis (and great bar food) to a twenty-something crowd. ⊛ 1321 W. Taylor St.
• Map H6 • Free

Beviamo Wine Bar
This dark, intimate Little Italy hideaway is a great place to cozy as a couple before or after dinner with one of 40 by-the-glass wines, or a "sampling flight" of three wines. ⊛ 1358 W. Taylor St. • Map H6
• Free • Closed Sun

Vernon Park Tap
Also known as Tu fano's, this popular bar counts legions of local and celebrity fans who pile in for house wine and generous, inexpensive pastas. ⊛ 1073 W. Vernon Park Pl. • Map H5 • Free • Closed Mon

Hawkeye's Bar & Grill
Try this sports bar for beer-fueled camaraderie and a genuine slice of Chicago fan zeal. A shuttle bus even delivers patrons to the United Center and US Cellular Field. ⊛ 1458 W. Taylor St. • Map H6 • Free • No DA

Unless otherwise specified bars and clubs charge admission, are open nightly, and have DA.

Price Categories

Price categories include a three-course meal for one, a glass of house wine, tax, and a 15-20% tip.	**$** under $20
	$$ $20–$30
	$$$ $30–$45
	$$$$ $45–$60
	$$$$$ over $60

Phoenix

🔟 Places to Eat

1 Phoenix
Phoenix attracts dim sum diners from near and far. Go early on weekends or prepare for long waits. ◈ *2131 S. Archer Ave.* • *Map A6* • *312-328-0848* • *$$*

2 Opera
Trendsetter Opera serves contemporized Chinese food in a former 1930s warehouse. Don't miss the five-spice squid and slow-braised pork. ◈ *1301 S. Wabash Ave.* • *Map K6* • *312-461-0161* • *Closed lunch* • *$$$$*

3 Gioco
Rustic Italian food is the draw at this stylish restaurant and one-time speakeasy. ◈ *1312 S. Wabash Ave.* • *Map K6* • *312-939-3870* • *Closed lunch Sat & Sun* • *$$$$*

4 Lao Szechuan
Located in the Chinatown Square shopping mall, this simple eaterie serves authentic Chinese Szechuan cuisine. ◈ *2172 S. Archer Ave.* • *Map C5* • *312-326-5040* • *$*

5 Chez Joel
A quaint French bistro in the heart of Little Italy charms fans with its sunny decor and fine classics like steak au poivre. ◈ *1119 W. Taylor St.* • *Map H6* • *312-226-6479* • *Closed lunch Sat, Sun & Mon* • *$$$$*

6 Pompei Bakery
A top Little Italy lunch pick, Pompeii showcases a dozen varieties of square, by-the-slice pizzas. Hot sandwiches and stuffed pastas round out the offerings. ◈ *1531 W. Taylor St.* • *Map H6* • *312-421-5179* • *No reservations* • *$*

7 Francesca's on Taylor
The Little Italy branch of Wrigleyville's Mia Francesca offers generous portions of refined Italian cuisine at reasonable prices. ◈ *1400 W. Taylor St.* • *Map H6* • *312-829-2828* • *Closed lunch Sat & Sun* • *$$$*

8 Rosebud Cafe
Its Italian cooking isn't daring but Rosebud's convivial vibe is hard to resist. Long waits for tables are common. ◈ *1500 W. Taylor St.* • *Map H6* • *312-942-1117* • *Closed lunch Sun* • *$$$*

9 Chicago Firehouse
The menu at this former fire station is best at its most basic, including burgers and sandwiches. ◈ *1401 S. Michigan Ave.* • *Map L6* • *312-786-1401* • *Closed lunch Sat & Sun* • *$$$$*

10 Penang
Chicago's only Malaysian restaurant. Ask your server to recommend the best dishes on the menu. ◈ *2201 S. Wentworth Ave.* • *Map C5* • *312-326-6888* • *$$*

Unless otherwise stated, all restaurants recommend reservations, accept credit cards, have DA, and are open for lunch and dinner.

97

Left **South Shore Cultural Center** Right **University of Chicago Campus**

Far South

WITH MAGNIFICENT ARCHITECTURE, *interesting ethnic enclaves, and stand-out museums, Chicago's Far South encompasses districts such as Hyde Park and Kenwood that merit a journey off the beaten tourist track – despite being bordered to the south by some less-than-welcoming neighborhoods. Hyde Park and Kenwood began life as suburbs for the wealthy escaping the dirty city; today, this part of town is a fascinating melting pot of University of Chicago students and Mexican, Asian, African-American, and Indian residents. Recreation and leisure opportunities abound on spectacular tracts of green space, including the University of Chicago's Midway Plaisance and Jackson Park, site of the 1893 World's Columbian Exposition (see p19).*

🔟 Sights

1. Museum of Science and Industry
2. University of Chicago
3. DuSable Museum of African-American History
4. South Shore Cultural Center
5. Oriental Institute
6. Robie House
7. Kenwood Historic District
8. Washington Park
9. Osaka Japanese Gardens
10. University of Chicago Sculptures

Giant Heart, Museum of Science and Industry

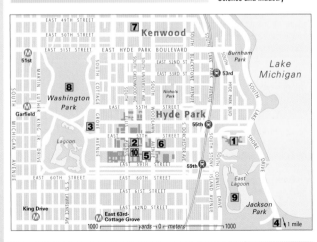

Museum of Science and Industry
The largest science museum within a single building in the Western Hemisphere, this museum attracts an amazing two million people a year *(see pp16–19)*.

University of Chicago
Noted for its research and high educational standards, this remarkable private university has produced over 70 Nobel Prize winners *(see pp28–9)*.

Annie Malone exhibit, Dusable Museum

DuSable Museum of African-American History
Located on the eastern edge of the beautiful Washington Park, this museum is named after Chicago's first non-native settler, Jean Baptiste Point du Sable. The permanent exhibits here celebrate other firsts, such as the first black US astronaut, Major Robert Lawrence, and Chicago's first and only African-American mayor, Harold Washington. Thought-provoking exhibits include rusted slave shackles and the "Freedom Now" mural, depicting 400 years of African-American history from the early days of slavery to Civil Rights marches. ✆ 740 E. 56th Pl. • Map D5 • Open 10am–5pm Tue–Sat, noon–5pm Sun • Adm. (free Sun) • DA

Bust (c. 1840 BC), Oriental Institute

South Shore Cultural Center
How ironic that this bustling arts and community center, which serves a largely African-American demographic, began in 1905 as an exclusive country club that barred minority members. Designed by the team who later worked on the elegant Drake Hotel *(see p115)*, this grand Mediterranean-style structure was bought and lovingly restored by the Chicago Park District when the country club fizzled out in the 1970s. Extravagant landscaping and flower beds complete the pretty picture, making it a popular spot for weddings and festivals, as well as for all kinds of performances and classes. Its golf course, nature park, and the public beach behind it add to its many draws. ✆ 7059 S. Shore Dr. • Map F6 • Open 9am–6pm Mon–Fri, 9am–5pm Sat • Free (except classes) • DA

Oriental Institute
Learn about the origins of agriculture, the invention of writing, the birth of civilization, and the beginning of the study of arts, science, politics, and religion at this University of Chicago departmental museum. Its five galleries showcase ancient Near Eastern civilizations from about 3500 BC to AD 100, and the exhibits were largely unearthed during the department's own excavations. ✆ 1155 E. 58th St. • Map E6 • 10am–6pm Tue–Sat (to 8:30pm Wed), noon–6pm Sun • Free • DA

Robie House

6 This splendid 1909 residence by Frank Lloyd Wright is easily spotted by its steel-beam roof, which over-hangs the building by 20 ft (6 m) at each end. Take a tour through its low-ceilinged interior,

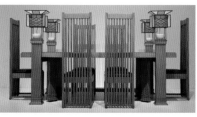

Frank Lloyd Wright tables and chairs in Robie House

and past more than 170 art-glass windows and doors, to gain insight into the ongoing, extensive ten-year restoration program. The building was a private home until 1926, when it became a dormitory for the Chicago Theo-logical Seminary. It was later bought by a development firm, who donated it to the Univer-sity of Chicago in 1963, the same year it was designated a National Historic Landmark. Ⓢ 5757 S. Woodlawn Ave. • Map E6 • Tours 11am, 1pm, 3pm Mon–Fri, every 30 min 11am–3:30pm Sat & Sun, call: 708-848-1976 • Adm. adults $12, children and seniors $10 • No DA

Kenwood Historic District

7 A world apart from some of the Far South's dicier areas, this wealthy enclave within Kenwood, founded by John A. Kennicott in 1856, has mansions that must be seen to be believed. In the late 19th century this area was an upscale Chicago suburb, where wealthy residents built majestic homes on spacious lots, a rarity in the quickly booming city. A stroll around the district uncovers architectural styles ranging from Italianate and Colonial Revival to Prairie style, by influential figures such as Howard Van Doren Shaw and Frank Lloyd Wright (see pp30–31). Ⓢ Boundaries: E. 43rd St. (north), E. 51st St. (south), S. Blackstone Ave. (east), and S. Drexel Blvd. (west) • Map E5

Detail of Taft's Fountain of Time, Washington Park

Washington Park

8 Frederick Law Olmsted and Calvert Vaux, the designers of New York's Central Park, also created this 371-acre (150-ha) green space for Chicago resi-dents in the early 1870s. It originally attracted mainly wealthy city dwellers who enjoyed parading around the scenic space. Today, it's a beautiful and widely used park with recreational programs, the DuSable Museum of African-American History, and Lorado Taft's striking 110-ft (34-m) long sculpture, Fountain of Time, which took him 14 years to build. It is unwise to venture into the park after dark. Ⓢ Map D5 • Open dawn–11pm (approx) • Free • DA

Osaka Japanese Gardens

9 At the north end of Jackson Park's serene Wooded Island (which is excellent for bird-watching), lies this hushed re-treat, complete with meandering paths, lagoons, and fountains. The extraordinary garden is a partial re-creation of the one formed in 1934 around the beautiful Japanese Pavilion that had been built for the 1893 Expo, but which sadly burned down in 1946. The gardens were renamed in 1993 for one of

Chicago's sister cities, Osaka, which donated the Japanese gate seen here. ◎ *Jackson Park, 58th St. & Lake Shore Dr.* • *Map F6* • *Open dawn–dusk* • *Free* • *DA*

10 University of Chicago Sculptures

Strolling around the University of Chicago campus, there's more of visual interest than its buildings alone. Over the years, the university has acquired around 12 outdoor sculptures, including Wolf Vostell's whimsical 1970 *Concrete Traffic*, a car embedded in concrete at the southwest end of the Midway Plaisance and the sobering *Nuclear Energy*, a bronze by Henry Moore that resembles a mushroom cloud. Set within a reflecting pool at 60th Street and University Avenue is *Construction in Space in the Third and Fourth Dimension*, a soaring abstract piece created in the 1950s by Constructivist Antoine Pevsner, which visually depicts the space-time continuum *(see p28–9).*

Osaka Japanese Gardens

Exploring Far South

Morning

Mingle with University of Chicago students over good coffee and great pancakes at the **Original Pancake House** *(see p103)*, where the sweet, baked Apple Dutch Baby is a must-try. From there, walk about a mile (1.6 km) south or hop on the no. 28 bus at the corner of Hyde Park Boulevard and Lake Park Avenue to visit the **Museum of Science & Industry** *(see pp16–19)*, where you can easily spend an engrossing few hours exploring the hands-on exhibits. For lunch, skip the museum food and head west about a mile (1.6 km) to **Medici** *(see p103)*, a great student and faculty hangout, known for its delicious pizzas. The extravagant Garbage Pizza is a favorite.

Afternoon

Stroll about four blocks southwest to the **Oriental Institute** *(see p99)* at the **University of Chicago** *(see pp28–9)* whose museum will transport you back to ancient times. Its Suq gift shop offers unique souvenirs, such as a replica of an ancient board game. Just east of the institute is Frank Lloyd Wright's masterpiece of Prairie-style architecture, **Robie House**. Take a tour of this to really gain some insight into the great man's vision. Then stroll around the university's leafy quadrangles if it's good weather, or backtrack a little to the **Smart Museum of Art** *(see p28)* if you'd rather be inside. Either way, round off your day with some good ol' home-style Southern cooking at the no-frills **Dixie Kitchen** *(see p103)*.

Left **Leather shoes, Collections** Right **House of Africa**

🔟 Shops

1 Powell's Bookstore
Here, used books in top condition are stacked floor to ceiling on painted wood shelves, with antique editions protected behind glass. ◎ *1501 E. 57th St. • Map E6*

2 Seminary Co-op Bookstore
Housed in the basement of the Chicago Theological Seminary on the University of Chicago campus, it's fitting that this bookstore has a well-respected academic section, especially humanities and social sciences. ◎ *5757 S. University Ave. • Map E5*

3 57th Street Books
This basement-level shop carries new fiction, children's books, and African-American interest titles. Low ceilings, brick walls, and a painted cement floor all create a cozy atmosphere, conducive to browsing. ◎ *1301 E. 57th St. • Map E6 • No DA*

4 The Co-op Market
Mingle with the melting pot of shoppers at this cooperative market, where aisles are dominated by organic, vegetarian, and international foodstuffs. ◎ *1526 E. 55th Street • Map E5*

5 House of Africa
The scent of sandlewood incense fills this small boutique that sells African artifacts, carved wooden sculptures, and CDs of music from all over the continent. ◎ *1352 E. 53rd St. • Map E5 • Closed Sun*

6 Alise's Designer Shoes
Shop for the latest men's and women's designer shoe fashions from Italy, France, Brazil, and the Far East, as well as ladies' bags, fine jewelry, and men's belts. ◎ *5210C S. Harper Ave. • Map F5*

7 Toys, Etc.
This inviting store focuses on non-violent toys galore. Good-old standbys include kites, face-painting kits, balls, and dress-up clothes. ◎ *5211 S. Harper Ave. • Map F5*

8 Little Black Pearl Workshop
The gift shop at this children's arts program and cultural arts center sells the students' amazing creations, such as one-of-a-kind painted furniture and vibrant mosaics. ◎ *1060 E. 47th St. • Map E5 • Closed Sun*

9 Collections
Chic club clothes and look-at-me leather shoes are sparsely displayed along the walls in this boutique. Many of the designs are straight off Italian runways, while others are custom-made by the shop's owner. ◎ *1360 E. 53rd St. • Map E5 • Closed Sun*

10 Artisans 21
This gallery showcases locally made art. You can purchase designs both to wear and to show, from whimsical ceramics to fringed silk scarves and handpainted jackets. ◎ *5225 S. Harper • Map F5 • No DA*

Most of these shops are usually open at least 10am–6pm Mon–Sat and noon–5pm Sun, and unless specified have DA

Price Categories

Price categories include a three-course meal for one, a glass of house wine, tax, and a 15–20% tip.

$	under $20
$$	$20–$30
$$$	$30–$45
$$$$	$45–$60
$$$$$	over $60

Dixie Kitchen and Bait Shop

TOP 10 Places to Eat

1 La Petite Folie
An upscale French restaurant offering a fixed-price menu, as well as entrées featuring ingredients such as rabbit and quail. ◎ 1504 E. 55th St. • Map E5 • 1-773-493-1394 • Closed Mon, Sat & Sun lunch • $$$

2 Florian Caffé
This no-reservations hangout for pizza and pasta also specializes in mile-high cakes, rich with chocolate, strawberry, coconut, and thick frosting. ◎ 1450 E. 57th St. • Map E6 • 1-773-752-4100 • $$

3 Calypso Café
In this feel-good Caribbean joint, jerk chicken is a favorite, and Key Lime pie is the must-do dessert. ◎ 5211 S. Harper St. • Map H6 • 1-773-955-0229 • $$

4 Dixie Kitchen & Bait Shop
A taste of America's South, serving fried catfish, crawfish étouffée, and jambalaya in a setting reminiscent of an old bait shop. ◎ 5225 S. Harper Ave. • Map F5 • 1-773-363-4943 • $$

5 Medici on 57th
Great pizza draws the crowds, but sandwiches on home-baked bread and rich milkshakes are also offered. ◎ 1327 E. 57th St. • Map E6 • 1-773-667-7394 • $$

6 Cedars of Lebanon
Delicious falafel, lamb kebobs, hummus, and dozens of other Middle Eastern dishes will fill you up for next to nothing at this BYO spot. ◎ Kimbark Plaza, 1618 E. 53rd St. • Map E5 • 1-773-324-6227 • $

7 Nile Restaurant
The extensive menu at this Middle Eastern diner makes decisions difficult, but combination plates let you try an assortment. ◎ 1611 E. 55th St. • Map E5 • 1-773-324-9499 • $ • No DA

8 Woodlawn Tap
A casual dress code, good food, and cheap beer attract all types to this bar especially for burgers and hearty soup. ◎ 1172 E. 55th St. • Map E5 • 1-773-643-5516 • $$

9 Mellow Yellow
This laid-back eatery offers specialties of rotisserie chicken and sweet or savory crepes. There's also a separate bar. ◎ 1508 E. 53rd St. • Map E5 • 1-773-667-2000 • $

10 Original Pancake House
This homey breakfast haven does everything well, but its signature dish is the apple pancake. ◎ 1517 E. Hyde Park Ave. • Map E5 • 1-773-288-2322 • Closed dinner • $

Around Town – Far South

Unless otherwise stated, all restaurants recommend reservations, accept credit cards, have DA, and are open for lunch and dinner.

Left **Christmas lights** Center **Wrapping up warmly** Right **Spring Tulips, Magnificent Mile**

Top 10 Planning Your Trip

1 When to Go
For a moderate climate the best time to visit is spring or fall. But if you can bear the snow and bitter cold of the festive season you'll see Chicago sparkle with magical Christmas lights – and you'll have a lot fewer tourists to contend with. Summer sees street festivals and live music in the parks. Avoid November visits, as the city's hotels are filled by conventioneers during this month.

2 Weather
Chicago winters are usually intemperate with heavy snow and temperatures ranging from 13° F (-9° C) to 37° F (4° C). Summer days can be anything from balmy to boiling, averaging 69° F (22° C) to 84° F (30° C). Extremes, like winter blizzards, heavy spring rains, and summer heat waves are not uncommon, with spring-time weather being particularly changeable. Despite the winds that can gust off Lake Michigan, Chicago's "Windy City" moniker is actually attributed to the verbose bid the city made to host the 1893 World's Columbian Exposition *(see p19)*.

3 What to Pack
Pack lightly for summer, and bring layers for the unpredictable spring and fall conditions. Layers are best for the often desperately cold winters, in order to cope with centrally heated environments. A hat and suitable footwear are essential then too. While casual clothes are acceptable in most places, men should bring a jacket and tie, since they are required at many upscale restaurants.

4 Insurance
It is strongly recommended to have a comprehensive travel insurance policy, including coverage for trip cancellation, lost luggage, car rental insurance and, most of all, medical expenses, which are very high in America.

5 Passports & Visas
Citizens of European Union countries, New Zealand, Australia, and Japan can spend up to 90 days in the US without a visa. They just need a valid passport and a round-trip ticket. Canadian citizens must only show photo ID and proof of residence. Citizens of other countries should contact their local US embassy well in advance of their trip to obtain the relevant visa.

6 Money
Do bring some dollars with you for essentials on arrival. But from then on, major credit cards are accepted in most places. ATMs abound, but check with your own bank to avoid the extra fee charged for using ATMs of non-affiliated US banks. It's also worthwhile bringing a few US dollar traveler's checks in case of emergency. These can be changed at most banks and foreign exchange on showing photo ID, and can also be used in stores and restaurants.

7 Driver's License
Foreign or out-of-state driver's licenses are valid in Chicago – if they are in English. Bring your picture license even if you don't plan to rent a car: it's a good alternative to a passport if you are asked for proof of age in a bar.

8 Electric Current & Phone Adapters
Electrical appliances in US operate on 110–120 volts and use two-prong plugs. This means that non-US, single-voltage appliances need an adapter and transformer, available in airport shops, and at many electrical stores and large department stores.

9 Discounts
If you have student or senior ID, it's a good idea to carry it with you to make the best of discounts offered on everything from public transit and hotels to admission to the main attractions.

10 Time Zone
Chicago operates on Central Time (six hours behind GMT). Daylight saving begins at 3am on the first Sunday in April and reverts to standard time at 1am on the last Sunday in October.

Left **Blue Line Train sign** Center **Amtrak train** Right **O'Hare Airport**

⑩ Arriving in Chicago

1 O'Hare International Airport

One of the world's busiest airports, O'Hare lies 20 miles (32 km) northwest of downtown Chicago. Serving most major airlines, this airport is big and spread out. Use the free Airport Transport System (ATS) to access the three domestic terminals, the international terminal, parking areas, and the Chicago Transit Authority (CTA) (see p108) station. ☏ 1-800-832-6352, www.ohare.com

2 Connections from O'Hare

Taxis are available on a first come first served basis from the lower level of the Arrivals terminal. Out of rush hours it can take around 45 minutes to reach Downtown. Car rental agencies are also at hand, near the baggage claim areas in terminals 1–3, and via courtesy telephones from terminal 5. Alternatively, shuttle buses, limos, and trains can take you into Chicago. For the latter, follow the "Trains to City" signs to the CTA Blue Line, the cheapest and – at 40 minutes – often the quickest way into town.

3 Midway Airport

Located 10 miles (16 km) southwest of Downtown, this recently renovated airport serves mostly budget airlines, as well as a few major ones. Taxis are available from exit M5; car rental agencies are located in the main terminal building; and shuttle buses leave from in front of it. Alternatively, follow signs from the terminal to the CTA station: the Orange Line brings you downtown in less than 30 minutes. ☏ 1-773-838-0600

4 Immigration

Landing cards and customs forms are distributed on the plane. Foreign nationals have to join a separate line to have these and their passports inspected after landing. Strict security checks, involving the taking of photographs and fingerprints, are now in place for those arriving in the US on a visa.

5 Shuttle Buses

These operate from both airports. Continental Airport Express will drop off at (and pick up from) any requested downtown location; Omega Airport Shuttle buses operate between the two airports. To catch a shuttle, go to the information counter at Baggage Claims. ☏ *Continental Airport Express: 1-888-284-3826 • Omega Airport Shuttle: 1-773-483-6634*

6 Limousines

Several limo companies, including Amm's and Chicago Express Limousine, offer private door-to-door services: book 24 hours in advance. Rates are higher than taxi fares, and tips should be 10–15%. ☏ *Amm's: 1-773-792-1126 • Chicago Express Limousine: 1-800-527-2137*

7 Car Rental

You usually have to be over 25 with a valid license to rent a car. Reputable agencies such as Avis (800-331-1212) and Hertz (800-654-3131) are at both main airports and throughout the city. A deposit will be required. Collision damage waiver and liability insurance are highly recommended.

8 By Train

Over 40 Amtrak trains serve Union Station each day. The nearest El stop is at Clinton, but it's a good walk, so it is often better to take a cab or bus to your destination. ☏ *210 S. Canal St., 1-800-872-7245*

9 By Bus

Catch long-distance buses from Greyhound's main downtown terminal. Then catch a cab to your destination, or walk one block north to take the El from Clinton station. ☏ *630 W. Harrison St., 1-800-231-2222*

10 By Car

Interstate highways into Chicago are I-55 from the southwest, I-57 from the south, I-88 from the west, I-90 from the east and northwest, and I-94 from the east and north. Route 66 from Santa Monica, CA joins I-55 before hitting Downtown.

Left **Water Taxi** Center **Trolley Bus** Right **Cyclists on the lakefront path**

🔟 Getting Around

1 The El

Short for elevated train, the El is nevertheless the name given to the entire CTA-run train network, including the sections that travel underground. The five major and three minor lines are identifiable by color: red, green, blue, brown, orange, pink, purple, and yellow. Some lines run 24 hours a day (less often off-peak). Trains arrive every 5–20 minutes, and the service is fast and economical.
✆ CTA: 773-836-7000
www.transitchicago.com

2 Buses

The CTA also operates an extensive network of buses, especially useful for reaching the lakefront, which is not served by the El. Look for the blue and white stops. Some also serve PACE buses that cover the city suburbs and are numbered 208 and higher.
✆ CTA: as above • PACE: 1-847-364-7223
www.pacebus.com

3 CTA transit cards & passes

A regular El or bus fare is $1.75, with an extra 25¢ for a transfer card (valid for two transfers within two hours of purchase), and you need exact change. However if you buy a Transit card with a preset value at a station ticket office, or get a top-up Transit card and charge it with the desired amount at a machine, the relevant fare is then deducted from your pass each time you take a ride. One- to five-day Visitor Passes are also available from stations, visitor centers, and selected tourist attractions.

4 Metra

Metra, the commuter rail system, serves the city's suburbs. Fares vary according to the journey's length. Downtown stops are Union Station, LaSalle Street Station, Ogilvie Transportation Center (see p37), and Randolph Street Station. ✆ Metra: 312-322-6777 (Mon–Fri) or 773-836-7000 (RTA Travel Information), www.metrarail.com

5 Taxis

It is usually easy to hail a cab Downtown; elsewhere it's better to call for one. There's an intial charge, then a fee per mile and per extra passenger. A 10–15% tip is expected. Companies include: ✆ Checker Taxi Assoc. 312-243-2537 • Flash Cab Co. 1-773-561-1444 • Yellow Cab Co. 312-829-4222

6 Water Taxis

In summer, Wendella Riverbus (312-337-1446) runs water taxis between the Wrigley Building and both Union Station and the Ogilvie Transportaion Center. Shoreline Water Taxi (312-222-9328) also offers a service every 20 minutes from Navy Pier (see pp20–21) to the John G. Shedd Aquarium and near the Sears Tower.

7 Trolley Buses

From Memorial Day to Labor Day (see 109), free daytime trolley buses run on four routes from downtown El and Metra stations to the Museum Campus, the Art Institute of Chicago, State Street and Michigan Avenue shopping areas, Navy Pier – and on weekends they run to Lincoln Park and Chinatown/Pilsen (see pp52–3). Look for the green and red Free Trolley signs.

8 Walking

Exploring most Downtown and Northside areas (such as the Mag Mile or Lincoln Park) on foot is fine. However, avoid walking south of the South Loop after dark.

9 Cycling

Only confident cyclists should consider city travel as the roads are so busy. However, the 18 miles (29 km) of lakefront bike paths are very pleasant. To get a Chicago Bike Map call 312-742-2453. Bike Chicago rents bikes and conducts bike tours from Navy Pier: call 1-800-915-2453 or visit www.bikechicago.com

10 Driving

Chicago's grid system (see street index), makes orientation relatively straightforward. However, expressways are often snarled, the Loop's one-way streets can be very confusing, and finding parking Downtown can be a huge, costly problem.

Left **No smoking sign** Center **Visitors Information center** Right **Disabled sign**

🔟 Useful Information

1 Information Centers

Chicago has two main tourist information centers: in the Chicago Cultural Center *(see p69)* and in the Historic Pumping Station *(see p26)*. Opening hours are at least 10am–6pm. You can also get further information by contacting the City of Chicago's Tourism Hotline (1-877-244-2246), the Chicago Convention and Tourism Bureau (312-201-8847), or the Illinois Bureau of Tourism (1-800-226-6632).

2 Websites

Information about Chicago can be found on several reliable websites, such as www.choose chicago.com and *www. 877chicago.com*. For in-depth reviews of where to go and what to see, log onto *www.metromix.com*, affiliated to the *Chicago Tribune*. Internet cafés include the national chain *Screenz* (773-348-9300).

3 Media

The city's two main daily newspapers are the *Chicago Tribune* and the *Chicago Sun-Times*. The most popular radio stations include: WNUA (95.5 FM) for jazz, WFMT (98.7 FM) for classical, WLUP (97.9 FM) for rock, and WGCI (107.5FM) for R&B. WBBM (780 AM) is a news station, and WSCR (670 AM) keeps you up to date on sports. For local TV, there's a wide range to choose from: CBS (Channel 2); NBC (Channel 5); ABC (Channel 7); WB (Channel 9); WTTW Public TV (Channel 11); and Fox (Channel 32).

4 Events

For a complete list of what's on in Chicago see www.877chicago.com, or pick up the Chicago *Reader* – a free paper that comes out every Thursday, available in restaurants, bars, and other venues. Chicago is known for its conventions, some so large that conventioneers almost take over the city. Check the "Convention Calendar" at *www.choose chicago.com*, to see if your visit coincides with any.

5 Tipping

Plan to tip for most services: waitstaff expect 15–20%; bell hops and porters $1 per bag; hotel maids about $2 per night; bartenders up to $1 a drink.

6 Telephones

Most public phones accept coins or phone cards (calls to Directory Assistance are free). Chicago has two area codes: 312 for downtown and the immediate vicinity; 773 for the rest of the city. Dial 1 plus the area code for any US number outside the area code you are in. To dial abroad, key 011 + country code + city code (omitting any initial 0). If you need to rent a cell phone, try *International Sound* (1-800-353-2100). AT&T, Nextel, and Sprint are the largest mobile networks.

7 Families & Disabled Visitors

Chicago Parent magazine (www.chicagoparent.com) has a monthly calendar of kids' activities. Information on disabled accessibility to the city's main attractions is published by the Mayor's office at www.accessible chicago.org.

8 Smoking & Drinking

Smoking is prohibited in many public spaces in Chicago, so check for no smoking signs before lighting up. The legal age for the purchase or consumption of alcohol is 21, and the law requires photo ID as proof.

9 Consulates

In emergencies, your consulate may give assistance. 🇦🇺 *Australia: 123 N. Wacker Dr., 312-419-1480*
• *Canada: 180 N. Stetson Ave., 312-616-1860*
• *Great Britain: Wrigley Building, 400 N. Michigan Ave., 312-970-3800*
• *Ireland: 400 N. Michigan Ave, 312-337-1868*

10 Public Holidays

New Year's Day (Jan 1); Martin Luther King Day (3rd Mon in Jan); President's Day (3rd Mon in Feb); Casimir Pulaski Day (1st Mon in Mar); Memorial Day (last Mon in May); Independence Day (July 4); Labor Day (1st Mon in Sep); Thanksgiving (4th Thu in Nov); Christmas Day (Dec 25).

Left **Lakefront recreation** Center **Hot Tix sign** Right **Public Art, North Michigan Avenue**

10 Chicago on a Budget

1 Free Admission Days
Several city attractions such as Lincoln Park Zoo *(see p24–5)* never charge admission. Others often have one free day per week: bear in mind it might be cheaper, but the crowds can be greater.

2 Free Events
Summer in Chicago brings sunshine and lots of free outdoor happenings, especially in Grant Park *(see p71)*. Arrive early to get a good spot, and bring a picnic and warm clothing for after the sun goes down. The Mayor's Office of Special Events and other sources of information *(see p109)* will have details of concerts, neighborhood festivals, parades, and more. ⚅ *Mayor's Office of Special Events (recorded info)* • *312-744-3370* • *www.cityof chicago.org/specialevents*

3 Free Tours
The Chicago Office of Tourism *(see p109)* provides information on a range of great free tours, such as the Cultural Center Tour and the Loop Tour Train *(see p111)*. The volunteer-run Chicago Greeters also offers an insider's take on the city at no charge *(see p111)*.

4 Dining Deals
Many restaurants have good-value "Early Bird Specials" or "pre-theater menus." Look for signs advertising deals.

5 Hot Tix
Half-price tickets for same-day theater performances can be bought in person at Hot Tix booths around the city. There is a slight discount for cash payment and a small fee for ticket processing. To save time fruitlessly waiting in line, check the website for daily listings of availability. ⚅ *Hot Tix: Chicago Cultural Center, 78 W. Randolph St.* • *Hot Tix: Waterworks Visitor Center 163 E. Pearson St.* • *Both closed Mon.* • *www.hottix.org*

6 Public Art
Many famous artists, such as Pablo Picasso and Marc Chagall, have left their artistic mark on the city. Details of public art Downtown are included in a booklet, the *Loop Sculpture Guide*, which is available at the Chicago Cultural Center and the Waterworks Visitor Center. The University of Chicago *(see pp28–9)* also has notable works on campus, while Navy Pier has sculpture displays during summer.

7 Parks & Recreation
Chicago's many beautiful parks are run by the Chicago Park District. Their excellent facilities include skating areas, beaches, pools, golf courses, tennis courts, and walking and cycling paths. Contact Bike Chicago *(see p111)* at Navy Pier to rent bikes or in-line skates. ⚅ *Chicago Park District: 312-742-7529, www.chicagoparkdistrict.com*

8 TV Audience Tickets
Free tickets for the *Oprah* and *Jerry Springer* shows are in demand, so call the hotlines at least a month in advance to avoid disappointment. Audience members generally have to be 18 years of age or over. ⚅ *Oprah: Harpo Studios, 1058 W. Washington St., 312-591-9222* • *Jerry Springer: NBC Tower, 454 N. Columbus Dr., 312-321-5365, www.studio audiences.com/daytime*

9 Special Promotions
Throughout the year, the Chicago Office of Tourism *(see p109)* offers several promotions, such as Winter Delights, which include discounts on lodging, attractions, and meals.

10 CityPass
This pass grants entry to the Museum Campus trio *(see p93)*; The Art Institute of Chicago; John Hancock Observatory; Museum of Science & Industry; Field Museum; and Shedd Aquarium. It can be purchased online or at any of the participating venues, and is valid for nine days from the first day of use. It offers substantial savings, and you don't have to wait in line. ⚅ *www.citypass.com*

Left **Uptown's Argyle Street Neighborhood** Center **Carriage Tours** Right **Lake Michigan Tours**

Tours & Cruises

1 Chicago Neighborhood Tours
Apart from tours of neighborhoods such as Chinatown and Bronzeville, this company also runs special interest bus trips (on themes like Chicago's theaters). Tours begin at the Chicago Cultural Center (see p69): call ahead to book. ⦿ Chicago Neighborhood Tours: 312-742-1190, www.chgocitytours.com

2 Chicago Architectural Foundation Tours
Learn about the city's amazing architecture on a Chicago Architecture Foundation (CAF) walking, bike, bus, or (in summer) boat tour. The fascinating trips highlight both historic and modern buildings, including Frank Lloyd Wright's architectural legacy. ⦿ CAF: 224 S. Michigan Ave., 312-922-8687, www.architecture.org

3 Bike Chicago Tours
Bike Chicago will guide you through the city's beautiful parks, neighborhoods, or along the stunning lakefront departing from either of its two locales. ⦿ Navy Pier: 600 E. Grand Ave., 312-595-9600 • North Avenue Beach • www.bikechicago.com

4 Untouchable Tours
Follow the trails of some of the city's most infamous 1920s and '30s gangster residents. Sites visited on this two-hour

tour include that of the St. Valentine's Massacre, Little Italy, and other haunts of the likes of Al Capone and John Dillinger. ⦿ Untouchables: 1-773-881-1195, www.gangstertour.com

5 Kayak Tours
Exercise your mind and your muscles by kayaking down the Chicago River while learning about the city's history and architecture. There are gangster and ghost themed tours for both beginners and advanced paddlers. ⦿ Wateriders Adventure Agents: 312-953-9287, www.wateriders.com

6 Lake & River Boat Tours
Join a narrated tour from the Lake or Wendella boat tour to gain historical or architectural insight from a different perspective. Metro Ducks offer a wackier take with their tours onboard an amphibious WWII craft. ⦿ Lake Boat Tours: 312-527-1977, www.chicagoline.com • Wendella Boats: 312-337-1446, www.wendellaboats.com • Metro Ducks: 1-800-298-1506, www.metroducks.com/chicago

7 Chicago Greeters
Run by the Chicago Office of Tourism (see p109), this free service gives groups of 1 to 6 visitors a chance to benefit from the wisdom of enthusiastic local residents who know and love the city. Choose

from a range of themed or neighborhood tours, and preferably book online seven days in advance. ⦿ 312-744-8000, www.chicagogreeter.com

8 Loop Train Tour
While circling the Loop (see pp68–75) on an El train (see p69) an expert from the CAF explains the history of significant buildings and the El itself. Free tickets are available at the Chicago Cultural Center (see p69) information desk on a first-come, first-served basis each day. ⦿ www.architecture.org, Sat only, May–Sept • DA

9 Carriage Tours
For a romantic ride along the waterfront, the Mag Mile, or around the Gold Coast area, book a traditional horse-drawn carriage. A flat fee is charged for a half-hour tour. ⦿ Antique Coach & Carriage: 1-773-735-9400, www.antiquecoachcarriage.com

10 Lake Cruises
Enjoy a meal or cocktails and dancing onboard the elegant Odyssey or Spirit of Chicago cruisers. In summer, schooners Windy I and Windy II, also sail on the breeze. All depart from Navy Pier. ⦿ Odyssey: 1-888-741-0281, www.odysseycruises.com • Spirit of Chicago: 312-836-7899, www.spiritcruises.com • Windy I & II: 312-595-5555, www.tallshipwindy.com

Check with tour operators as many tours are seasonal.

Left **Osco Drug store** Center **Lake front in Winter** Right **Police**

TOP 10 Tips on Health & Security

Preventing Theft
As in most cities, the most common crimes are pickpocketing and purse snatching. Common sense can help deter these problems. Leave surplus cash, unnecessary credit cards, and valuables in a safe place at your hotel. Don't walk around with your wallet in a back pocket, and keep bags securely fastened and close to your body. Do keep a copy of your credit card numbers (and the number to call if they are lost) separate from the cards, and bring photocopies of important documents in case they are stolen.

Public Transport
It's best to avoid using public transportation late at night. Take a taxi instead. However, when you do take a train, stand well back on the platform until the train has stopped, never sit in an empty carriage, and do not lean against the train doors. Train platforms and trains usually have an intercom in case of emergency.

Knowing Your Surroundings
Plan your route before setting off so that you know where you are going. If you do get lost, try not to make a big show of consulting your map or guidebook. At night, avoid walking alone in dimly lit areas and in parks. Steer clear of areas beyond the south branch of the Chicago River (west of Downtown) and parts of the South Side where crime levels are higher.

Hotel Room Safety
Make yourself aware of the fire escape route from your room as soon as you arrive. Always keep the door locked, and be sure you know who is knocking before you let anyone in. Valuables are best kept locked in the in-room, or preferably hotel, safe.

Telephone Hotlines
For police, fire, and medical emergencies call 911. If you are not in a position to speak, the emergency locator should still be able to track you. For non-emergency police matters, such as theft, dial 311 to reach the City Helpline. Both numbers can be accessed by cell phones.

Hospitals
Hospitals and emergency rooms are listed in the Yellow Pages of the telephone directory. Your concierge will know which one is most convenient. Weiss Memorial Hospital and Northwestern Memorial Hospital are convenient to Downtown and the Northside of the city, while Bernard A. Mitchell Hospital, at The University of Chicago, serves the South Side. ◎ *Weiss Memorial Hospital: 4646 N. Marine Dr., Map B3, 1-773-878-8700*

• *Northwestern Memorial Hospital: 251 E.Erie St., Map L2, 312-926-5188* • *The University of Chicago's Bernard A. Mitchell Hospital: 5815 S. Maryland Ave., Map E6, 1-773-702-1000*

Medical Emergencies
In an emergency, call 911 or go directly to the nearest hospital. Even with medical insurance, you may have to pay for services yourself and claim reimbursement after. Contact your insurer before receiving any treatment.

Dental Emergencies
Many dental clinics are open 24 hours. Check with the hotel concierge or contact the Chicago Dental Society for a referral. ◎ *Chicago Dental Society: 312-836-7300*

Pharmacies
Pharmacies are plentiful throughout the city. Many are open 24 hours. The most popular drug store chains (Walgreens, Osco, and CVS) all have pharmacies inside.

Seasonal Hazards
Chicago is a city of extreme seasons. Visitors should be prepared for cold, windy, and snowy winters, which can create hazardous conditions. In summer, the extreme heat can cause health problems: ensure you apply sunscreen, wear a hat, and drink plenty of water.

Left **Broadway Antique Market** Right **Water Tower Place**

Streetsmart

🔟 Shopping Tips

1 Store Hours
Regular store and mall hours are usually 10am to 9pm, Monday to Saturday, and 11am to 6pm Sunday. However, Northside boutiques and stores along the Mag Mile (see pp26–7) often stay open 'til 7–8pm.

2 Taxes
Chicago state and local sales taxes are among the highest in the country at 9 percent on all non-food items.

3 Sales Periods
Some Chicago stores have items on sale all year round, but expect real bargains after Christmas, on Presidents' Day, and on Labor Day (see p109).

4 Department Stores
You're in shopper's heaven when it comes to department stores in Chicago, which are mostly located on North Michigan Avenue and State Street. They include upscale Macy's (see p74), practical Sears (see p74), traditional Lord & Taylor, and stylish Bloomingdale's Home & Furniture Store (see p59). ⊗ Lord & Taylor: Water Tower Place, 835 N. Michigan Ave.
• Bloomingdale's: 900 N. Michigan Ave.

5 Shopping Malls
There's no shortage of malls in the city, especially vertical ones on the Mag Mile. Here you'll find Water Tower Place (see p26); Westfield North Bridge (see pp56–7); Chicago Place – featuring the Midwest's flagship Saks Fifth Avenue – and 900 North Michigan Shops. Regular malls are scattered all around the city and its suburbs. ⊗ Chicago Place: 700 N. Michigan Ave.

6 Chicago Souvenirs
Accent on Chicago and the City of Chicago Store have shelves filled with Chicago mementos (see p59). Authentic local food such as pizza and Eli's cheesecake can be shipped anywhere in the US by Taste of Chicago. ⊗ Accent on Chicago: 875 N. Michigan Ave. • City of Chicago Store: Chicago Waterworks Visitors Center, 163 E. Pearson St. • Taste of Chicago: 1-877-908-2783, www.tastesofchicago.com

7 Discount Outlets
Look for real bargains at Filene's Basement, while higher-end men's and women's clothing are discounted in the Mark Shale and Gap stores. Good value jewelery can be found at the Jeweler's Center (see p74), and cheap housewares at Crate & Barrel. ⊗ Filene's Basement: 1 N. State St./ 830 N. Michigan Ave.
• Mark Shale Outlet: 2593 Elston Ave. • Gap Outlet: 2778 N. Milwaukee Ave.
• Crate & Barrel Outlet: 1864 N. Clybourn Ave.

8 Music & Books
Borders and Barnes & Noble bookstores are all over the city. But for specialty books and personal service, try the Savvy Traveller or Sandmeyer's Bookstore. The Virgin Megastore looks cool inside, but for great value CDs check out the back wall racks of the legendary Rolling Stones shop, or go to Reckless Records for used vinyl.
⊗ Savvy Traveller: 310 S. Michigan Ave.
• Sandmeyer's Bookstore: 714 S. Dearborn St.
• Virgin Megastore: 540 N. Michigan Ave.
• Rolling Stones: 7300 W. Irving Pk. Rd.
• Reckless Records: 3161 N. Broadway

9 Art & Antiques
For information on art exhibitions, get a copy of Chicago Gallery News, which is available at visitor centers, or head to the River North Gallery District (see p79). Taylor's Guide to Antique Shops in Illinois and Southern Wisconsin (available in bookstores or by calling 1-847-465-3314) will direct you to the best local antique dealers.

10 Size Conversions
Clothing and shoe sizes in the UK, Europe, and the US differ, and conversions are complicated. Look at www.online conversion. com for help with sizes.

113

Left **Continental Breakfast, Chicago style** Right **Pizzeria Uno**

Accommodation & Dining Tips

1 Booking a Room
To book a room, contact the Chicago Convention and Tourism Bureau (CCVB). Discounted rates *(see below)* can be found by checking the Internet on sites such as *www. 877chicago.com*, calling the hotel directly, or contacting a reputable, no-fee reservation service such as Hot Rooms and Hotel Reservations Network. To hold a reservation, a credit card is usually necessary: no-shows will be charged. Be sure to specify if you want a smoking or non-smoking room.
§ *CCVB: 1-877-244-2246, www.choosechicago.com • Hot Rooms: 1-800-468-3500, www.hotrooms.com*

2 Rates
Hotel rates vary according to the hotel category, and the time of week and season. Peak rates are weekdays and from April–December. Rack rates, the basic room rates, are the ones used in this book to provide a guide price. Don't settle for them! It is almost always possible to get a better deal, so don't be too shy to ask.

3 Rooms
Usually, the larger the room, the higher the tab, and many, though not all, hotels charge more for a room with a view – so consider how much time you will want to spend in your room

before you pay the premium. Twin-bedded rooms are uncommon; most double rooms have either a queen- or king-sized bed or two double beds. If staying in a busy area, check to make sure rooms are soundproof.

4 Bed & Breakfasts
Bed & Breakfasts are a great way to see the city from a different perspective. For a list of homes offering guest rooms, check with At Home Inn Chicago, or Illinois Bed & Breakfast Association (ILBBA). Many require a minimum stay of two nights. § *At Home Inn Chicago: 1-312-640-1050, 800-375-7084 (toll free) • www.athomeinnchicago.com • ILBBA: 1-888-523-2406 • www.bbonline.com*

5 Taxes
Downtown restaurants add on a 9.5 percent local sales tax to your check, and hotel tax in Chicago is quite high at 15.4 percent (though the suburbs are slightly cheaper). Room rates tend to be quoted without tax.

6 Restaurant Reservations
Some restaurants do not take reservations (or only for groups of more than five), while for others, in particular the upscale ones, reservations well in advance are a must, especially on weekends. We indicate a recommendation for the

restaurants listed in this book, but it is always a good idea to call and check, especially if you have special needs or dietary requirements.

7 Meal Times
Breakfast is usually served in diners and coffee shops from about 6–10am. Lunch is normally available from 11:30am–2pm, and dinner takes place between approximately 5–10pm depending on the establishment. Early-bird dinners, normally served from 5–7pm, are usually a good bargain.

8 Chicago-Style & Ethnic Cuisine
Deep-dish pizza, hot dogs, and steaks are Chicago's main specialties. But in a city where a multitude of cultures meet, so do a multitude of cuisines, so check out the city's many ethnic restaurants *(see p42–3)*.

9 Portions
You will find that portions vary hugely from place to place. Often portions at upscale restaurants are smaller, while steakhouses and ethnic eateries offer a more than generous serving.

10 Dress Codes
Few restaurants have strict dress codes, though some hotel and other upscale restaurants still expect men to wear jackets and ties.

Price Categories	
For a standard, double room per night (with breakfast if included), taxes and extra charges.	$ under $100
	$$ $100–200
	$$$ $200–300
	$$$$ $300–400
	$$$$$ over $400

Peninsula Chicago

🔟 Luxury Hotels

1 Ritz-Carlton
The Ritz has it all – superior service, an award-winning dining room, spa, and state-of-the-art-business facilities. Impressive views complement the classic furnishings and fine art in its spacious guest rooms, but it's the little things, like Bulgari toiletries and toys and cookies for the kids that puts it in a league of its own. 🚇 *160 E. Pearson St. • Map L2 • 312-266-1000 • www.fourseasons.com • $$$$$*

2 Four Seasons
Expect the best in this grand hotel – possibly Chicago's most elegant. Lavish rooms command sweeping city and lake views, and the award-winning Seasons restaurant is a must try. 🚇 *120 E. Delaware Pl. • Map K2 • 312-280-8800 • www.fourseasons.com • $$$$$*

3 Peninsula Chicago
Understated elegance sums up this hotel. Large, earth-toned rooms have dressing areas, and a steam-free TV screen and hands-free telephone is found in every bathroom. Floor-to-ceiling windows dramatize the lobby, where afternoon tea is accompanied by live classical music. 🚇 *108 E. Superior St. • Map L2 • 312-337-2888 • http://fasttrack. chicago.peninsula.com • $$$$$*

4 The Drake
Popular with visiting celebrities and royalty, this is the grande dame of Chicago hotels, which effortlessly blends modern convenience with the charm of days gone by. Each of the 535 tastefully decorated rooms and suites is unique: many offer breathtaking views. 🚇 *140 E. Walton Pl. • Map L2 • 312-787-2200 • www.thedrakehotel.com • $$$–$$$$$*

5 Sofitel Chicago Water Tower
This sleek, striking, ultra-modern hotel opened in 2003. Spectacular views, sumptuous feather beds, and private baths and showers feature in every room. Plus there is a 24-hour fitness center. 🚇 *20 E. Chestnut St. • Map K2 • 312-324-4000 • www. sofitel.com • $$$–$$$$$*

6 Park Hyatt
Original contemporary art, rich woods, and warm tones create comfortable and tranquil public and private areas at this elegant boutique hotel. The state-of-the-art rooms feature furniture designed by Mies van der Rohe. 🚇 *800 N. Michigan Ave. • Map L2 • 312-335-1234 • www.park chicago.hyatt.com • $$$$$*

7 Fairmont
Overlooking Grant Park and Lake Michigan, the Fairmont features large, comfortably furnished rooms that include high-speed internet access, dressing areas, and marble bathrooms. 🚇 *200 N. Columbus Dr. • Map L4 • 312-565-8000 • www. fairmont.com • $$–$$$$*

8 Renaissance Chicago Hotel
On the south bank of the Chicago River, this 27-storey hotel affords amazing city views. Inviting guest rooms feature muted colors and warm woods, and there are spa packages available for men and women. 🚇 *1 W. Wacker Dr. • Map K3 • 312-372-7200 • www.renaissancehotels.com • $$$$*

9 InterContinental Chicago
One of the city's most luxurious hotels, which mixes historic charm with contemporary elegance. This former men's club (see p27) has stunning public rooms, including a swimming pool, and very comfortable guest rooms. 🚇 *505 N. Michigan Ave. • Map L2 • 312-944-4100 • www.chicago.inter continental.com • $$$$*

10 Conrad Chicago
Simple elegance and contemporary décor are features of this luxury hotel. In addition to 311 guestrooms and suites, there is The Restaurant at Conrad, The Terrace at Conrad, and Rendez-Vous (a stylish lounge). 🚇 *521 N. Rush St. • Map L2 • 312-645-1500 • www.conrad hotels.com • $$$*

Unless otherwise stated, all hotels accept credit cards, have private bathrooms, air con, non-smoking rooms, and rooms with DA

115

Left **The Hilton Chicago** Right **Guest room, Hotel Burnham**

TOP 10 Historic Hotels

1 The Hilton Chicago
When it opened in 1927 The Hilton was the world's largest hotel. Popular with US presidents, it oozes opulence – especially the Versailles-inspired Grand Ballroom. The Executive Class King Lakeview rooms offer the best views. 📍 720 S. Michigan Ave. • Map L6 • 312-922-4400 • www.chicagohilton.com • $$$

2 Palmer House Hilton
Palmer House, recently renovated, has been an elegant fixture in the heart of the Loop for over 125 years. Extravagant frescoes decorate the ornate lobby's ceiling, while the guest rooms are subtly elegant. The hotel even has its own upscale shopping arcade. 📍 17 E. Monroe St. • Map L4 • 312-726-7500 • www.chicagohilton.com • $$

3 Hotel Burnham
The Reliance Building – a handsome example of the Chicago School of architecture (see pp36–7) – was reborn as the boutique Hotel Burnham in 1999. Plush rooms are decorated in gold and blue, some with great views. A complimentary wine reception is held every evening. 📍 1 W. Washington St. • Map J4 • 312-782-1111 • www.burnhamhotel.com • $$$$–$$$$$

4 Omni Ambassador East
In its heyday, this lavish hotel hosted stars such as Frank Sinatra and Liza Minelli. Comfortable rooms sport dark wood furniture and chintz furnishings; public areas, such as the Pump Room (see p83), are more impressive. 📍 1301 N. State Pkwy. • Off map • 312-787-7200 • www.omnihotels.com • $$

5 The Talbott
Enjoy the quiet elegance of this small, family-owned, European-style hotel. The Victorian parlor-like lobby and atmospheric Basil's bar and café offer a chance to unwind, and the 149 guest rooms and suites are large and welcoming. 📍 20 E. Delaware Pl. • Map K2 • 312-944-4970 • www.talbotthotel.com • $$$

6 Allerton Hotel
Originally a residential hotel, the Allerton has a high-ceilinged, 1940s-inspired lobby, and large, traditional guest rooms with marble baths and lots of amenities. Don't miss the panorama from the 25th floor. 📍 701 N. Michigan Ave. • Map L2 • 312-440-1500 • www.sixcontinentshotels.com • $$–$$$

7 The Whitehall
A quiet, understated European ambience has permeated this hotel since it opened in 1928. The 221 guest rooms combine elegant tradition with mod cons, and the Presidential Suite was a favorite of Katherine Hepburn. Check out the Fornetto Mei restaurant with its menu of neo-Milanese cuisine and thin-crust specialty pizzas. 📍 105 E. Delaware Pl. • Map K2 • 312-944-6300 • www.whitehallhotel.com • $$–$$$

8 The Raphael
This former nurses' residence, built in the 1920s, now aptly bills itself as a quaint little hotel with old-world charm. The general effect is light and spacious, though some of the rooms and furnishings are a little tired. 📍 201 E. Delaware Pl. • Map K2 • 312-943-5000 • www.raphaelchicago.com • $$

9 The Tremont
An inviting fireplace welcomes you at this 1920s-built hotel, where guest rooms are small but comfortable; some have antique furniture and four-posters. Mike Ditka's restaurant is famous for its steaks and the collection of sports memorabilia. 📍 100 E. Chestnut St. • Map K2 • 312-751-1900 • www.tremontchicago.com • $$

10 Millennium Knickerbocker
This hotel, once owned by Playboy Magazine, has hosted guests as famous as John Kennedy and Al Capone. Its 1930s lobby holds the Martini Bar (with live music most days), and the guest rooms exude a timeless elegance. 📍 163 E. Walton Pl. • Map L2 • 312-751-8100 • www.millenniumhotels.com • $$$

Unless otherwise stated, all hotels accept credit cards, have private bathrooms, air con, non-smoking rooms, and rooms with DA

Left **Garden, Gold Coast Guest House B&B** Right **Wheeler Mansion**

Stylish Stays

1 W Chicago Lakeshore

A Zen water wall and "Leave me alone", rather than "Do not disturb" signs are indications of the W's hipper take on the hotel experience. The modern guest rooms have lovely views, as does the rooftop lounge, Whiskey Sky *(see p44)*. ✪ 644 N. Lake Shore Dr. • Map M3 • 312-943-9200 • www.whotels.com • $$$

2 Wheeler Mansion

An immaculate 11-room hotel, this 130-year-old mansion is known for its great attention to detail. Soak up the lavish artwork, period features, and antique furniture, or take it easy in the tranquil garden. ✪ 2020 S. Calumet Ave. • Off map • 312-945-2020 • www.wheeler mansion.com • $$$

3 House of Blues Hotel

This amazing hotel is much more than just somewhere to lay your head. A golden Buddha welcomes guests, and the atmospheric Kaz Bar has a Moroccan theme. State-of-the-art rooms offer hi-tech entertainment and eclectic decor. ✪ 333 N. Dearborn St. • Map K3 • 312-245-0333 • www.houseofblues.com • $$

4 W Chicago City Center

This hotel is trendy yet traditional, with comfy couches and board games in the lobby. Guest room decor is inspired by 1940s Hollywood glamor, with chaises longues and ostrich-leather headboards. ✪ 172 W. Adams St. • Map J4 • 312-332-1200 • www.whotels.com • $$$–$$$$

5 Hotel Monaco

Most of the luxe rooms in this stylish 14-story hotel feature window seats (a.k.a "secluded meditation stations"), while the spirit is further calmed by aromatherapy oils in the bathrooms. Pep things up in the Party Like a Rock Star Suite, complete with jukebox and Jacuzzi tub. ✪ 225 N. Wabash Ave. • Map K3 • 312-960-8500 • www.monaco-chicago.com • $$

6 Hotel Blake

This hotel contained printing presses before ever housing people. Now a National Historic Landmark, it offers large, light rooms. Savor Midwestern delicacies at the award-winning Custom House restaurant. ✪ 500 S. Dearborn St. • Map K5 • 312-986-1234 • www.printersrow.hyatt.com • $$$

7 Crowne Plaza Silversmith

Built in 1897, this beautiful building incorporates both Romanesque Revival and Arts and Crafts styles. The large guest rooms have Frank Lloyd Wright-inspired furniture, high ceilings, and large windows. A complimentary dessert hour is offered Monday through Thursday for in-house guests. ✪ 10 S. Wabash Ave. • Map K4 • 312-372-7696 • www.crowneplaza.com • $$$

8 Hard Rock Hotel

This extravagant 381-room, musically themed hotel occupies the former Carbide and Carbon building – an Art Deco creation of 1929. Piped music and memorabilia are everywhere, and rooms are stylish but fun. ✪ 230 N. Michigan Ave. • Map L2 • 312-345-1000 • www.hardrock.com • $$$

9 Hotel Allegro

Here, designer Cheryl Rowley has combined classic Art Deco features with contemporary colors and textures to great effect at this musically themed hotel. Complimentary wine is a standard nightly offering for guests. Fresh and fun. ✪ 171 W. Randolph St. • Map J4 • 312-236-0123 • www.hotelallegro chicago.com • $$$

10 Gold Coast Guest House B&B

This 1873 town house makes a pleasant change from the large hotels, with just four individually decorated rooms. Guests are welcome to use the comfortable sitting room and ivy-walled garden. ✪ 113 W. Elm St. • Map K1 • 312-337-0361 • www.bbchicago.com • No DA • $$

Left **Homewood Suites** Right **Lobby, Hilton Garden Inn**

 Budget Sleeps

1 Best Western Hawthorne Terrace

Warm and inviting sums up this 59-room hotel. An outdoor terrace overlooks the Lake View area, and guests can also use a small exercise room with sauna and whirlpool. Continental breakfast is included. ◎ 3434 N. Broadway • Map E2 • 1-773-244-3434 • www.hawthorne terrace.com • $$

2 Days Inn Lincoln Park North

This hotel is Chicago's highest-rated Days Inn. Free passes to the fitness center next door are part of the deal when you stay, as well as a continental breakfast and free wi-fi throughout the hotel. ◎ 644 W. Diversey Pkwy. • Map E2 • 1-773-525-7010 • www.lpndaysinn.com • $$

3 Belmont City Suites

A favorite of gangsters and mob bosses during Prohibition, this cozy, refurbished hotel now stands in the center of what makes Lakeview popular. Steps from Boys Town's Halsted Strip, this is a great choice for those who like city nightlife. ◎ 933 W. Belmont Ave.• Map E2 • 773-404-3400 • www.cityinns.com • $$

4 Embassy Suites Chicago:Downtown Lakefront

The impressive 13-story Sky Lobby offers a great place to unwind, with its soaring atrium. Glass-sided elevators whisk guests to suites with amenities that include high-speed Internet access and microwaves. Full American breakfast is also included. ◎ 511 N. Columbus Dr. • Map L4 • 1-888-903-8884 • www. chicagoembassy.com • $$$

5 The Inn at Lincoln Park

This hotel's Tudor-style exterior, Victorian lobby, and wagon-wheel trim are best described as eclectic. And while the rooms are definitely no-frills, the complimentary breakfast with views of Lincoln Park is a plus. ◎ 601 W. Diversey Pkwy. • Map E2 • 1-773-348-2810 • $–$$

6 Homewood Suites by Hilton

The two-room suites in this great value hotel all have fully equipped kitchens, as well as living rooms with extra queen-size sofa beds. Use of the 19th-floor indoor pool and the fitness center all add to your stay here. ◎ 40 E. Grand Ave. • Map L3 • 312-644-2222 • www.homewood suiteschicago.com • $$$

7 Hilton Garden Inn

Each of this hotel's functional and spacious 357 rooms offers a large desk, complimentary high-speed Internet access, and many other amenities. Six corner suites offer the perfect setup for families and groups of friends: the hotel also has a pool and gym. ◎ 10 E .Grand Ave. • Map L3 • 312-595-0000 • www.hiltongardeninn.com • $$$

8 Hampton Inn & Suites

This centrally located, family-friendly hotel offers two-room suites – with fully equipped kitchens – as well as many standard guest rooms. Bonuses include the fitness facility, indoor pool, complimentary breakfast buffet, and daily newspaper. ◎ 33 W. Illinois St. • Map K3 • 312-832-0330 • www. hamptoninn.com • $$$

9 Red Roof Inn Chicago

This is a great option for budget-minded travelers. Rooms at this centrally located inn are small, but they have all the essentials. A branch of the Coco Pazzo restaurant chain is on site. ◎ 162 E. Ontario St. • Map L2 • 312-787-3580 • www.redroof.com • $$

10 Hostelling International Chicago

This place is great value if you don't mind sleeping in a basic dormitory with local students, and you don't need to be a member in order to stay here. The facility includes lounges, fully equipped kitchens, and bed linen. ◎ 24 E. Congress Pkwy. • Map L5 • 312-360-0300 • www.hichicago.org • $

 Some budget accommodations offer weekday evening receptions with complimentary refreshments.

View of Atrium, Embassy Suites Chicago Downtown

TOP 10 Business-Friendly Stays

1 Sheraton Chicago Hotel & Towers

The large, stylish guest rooms here offer fantastic lake, city, or river views. The hotel also has its own business center, boat dock, health club, and five restaurants. Popular with conventioneers. ⬡ 301 E. North Water St. • Off map • 312-464-1000 • www.sheraton chicago.com • $$$

2 Westin Chicago River North

This sleek, four-star venue is home to a state-of-the-art Executive Business Center, fitness facility, and smoke-free guest rooms featuring the comfortable Westin Heavenly Bed. ⬡ 320 N. Dearborn Ave. • Map K3 • 312-744-1900 • www.westinrivernorth.com • $$$

3 Hyatt Regency McCormick Place

Linked by a connecting walkway to McCormick Place convention center, the basic but modern rooms of the 32-story Hyatt Regency are an attractive stopover for conventioneers. The hotel also has a fitness facility. ⬡ 2233 S. Martin Luther King Dr. • Map D5 • 312-567-1234 • www.mccormick place.hyatt.com • $$

4 Embassy Suites Hotel O'Hare-Rosemont

This hotel's seven-story garden atrium makes a pleasant retreat from the hustle and bustle of the nearby convention center and airport. Suites have all the necessary facilities; cooked breakfasts and an airport shuttle are complimentary. ⬡ 5500 N. River Rd., Rosemont • Off map • 1-847-678-4000 • www.embassyohare.com • $$$

5 Swissôtel

Rising up where the Chicago River and Lake Michigan meet is this dramatic glass-and-steel creation. Oversized guest rooms contain every convenience for the business traveller and provide stellar views of the city. ⬡ 323 E. Wacker Dr. • Map L3 • 312-565-0565 • www.swissotel.com • $$$

6 Hyatt Regency Chicago

A lobby full of greenery and fountains welcomes guests into this, the biggest hotel in the Hyatt chain. Although all guest rooms offer high speed Internet access, you can opt for a "Business Plan" upgrade to obtain more specific benefits during your stay. ⬡ 151 E. Wacker Dr. • Map L3 • 312-565-1234 • www.hyatt.com • $$$–$$$$

7 Chicago Marriott Downtown

This 46-story hotel's contemporary rooms are designed to cater to every business need. Guests can also enjoy the hotel's five restaurants and lounges, or its on-site pool and fitness center. ⬡ 540 N. Michigan Ave. • Map L2 • 312-836-0100 • www.marriott.com • $$$

8 Embassy Suites Hotel Chicago Downtown

The lofty atrium here is filled with plants, birds, and fountains; the two-room suites are spacious and well-equipped; service is personal; and cooked breakfasts plus other perks are included. ⬡ 600 N. State St. • Map K2 • 312-943-3800 • www.embassysuites.com • $$

9 Courtyard by Marriott Chicago Downtown

Bright, modern rooms with high speed Internet access, a spacious work area, and an extra sofa-bed make this centrally located hotel a popular choice among leisure and business travelers alike. ⬡ 30 E. Hubbard St. • Map K3 • 312-329-2500 • www.courtyard.com • $$

10 Hilton Chicago O'Hare Airport

The only hotel actually on airport grounds (conveniently linked to airport terminals via underground walkways) offers an enhanced business center, providing state-of-the-art telecommunications and multimedia conference facilities. Rooms are well sound-proofed. ⬡ O'Hare Airport • Map A3 • 1-773-686-8000 • www.hilton.com • $$$

Unless otherwise stated, all hotels accept credit cards, have private bathrooms, air con, non-smoking rooms, and rooms with DA

119

General Index

Index

Acknowledgements

The Authors

Chicago-based freelancer Elaine Glusac specializes in travel writing for an array of publications including *National Geographic Traveler* and the *International Herald Tribune*.

Elisa Kronish is a Chicago native who has written about the city's highlights and hidden finds for a variety of print and online travel guides such as Citysearch Chicago.

Roberta Sotonoff is a travel junkie. She writes about a variety of travel destinations, and her work has appeared worldwide in over 40 newspapers, magazines, on-line sites and guidebooks.

Produced by Departure Lounge, London
Editorial Director Naomi Peck
Art Director Lisa Kosky
Picture Researcher Debbie Woska
Editorial and Design Assistance Kelly Thompson, Davin Kuntze, Debbie Woska, Caroline Blake
Photographer Jim Warych
Additional Photography Andrew Leyerle
Illustrator Lee Redmond
Maps (DK India) Managing Editor: Aruna Ghose, Senior Cartographer: Uma Bhattacharya, Cartographers: Suresh Kumar, Alok Pathak
Proofreader Mary Sutherland
Factchecker Misty Tosh
Indexer Hilary Bird

AT DORLING KINDERSLEY
Publishing Managers Fay Franklin, Kate Poole
Senior Art Editor Marisa Renzullo
Publisher Douglas Amrine
Senior Cartographic Editor Casper Morris
DTP Jason Little, Conrad van Dyk
Production Controller Shane Higgins
Additional Contributions Emily Anderson, D Clancy, Robert Devendorf, Rada Radojicic, Brett Steel, Ros Walford

Picture Credits

t-top, tl-top left; tlc-top left centre; tc-top centre; tr-top right; cla-centre left above; ca-centre above; cra-centre right above; cl-centre left; c-centre; cr-centre right; clb-centre left below; cb-centre below; crb-centre right below; bl-bottom left, b-bottom; bc-bottom centre; bcl-bottom centre left; br-bottom right; d-detail.

Every effort has been made to trace the copyright holders, and we apologize for any unintentional omissions. We would be pleased to insert the appropriate acknowledgements in any subsequent editions of this publication.

Works of art have been reproduced with the permission of the following copyright holders: *Table and chairs Robbie House* Frank Lloyd-Wright © ARS, NY and DACS, London 2007 100tr.

The publishers would like to thank the following individuals, companies and picture libraries for their kind permission to reproduce their photographs.

20th CENTURY FOX: 61tr; ALAMY: Arcaid Ed 31tl; Edward Hattersley 4–5; Andre Jenny 66–67; Kim Karpeles 12crb; Jason Lindsey 32–33; Popperfoto 34c, 37d; ALAN KLEHR:14–15c, 76–77; ART INSTITUTE OF CHICAGO: 6cra, 8cb, 9c, 2tl, 9tl, 9cra, 10 bl; *American Gothic* Grant Wood, Friends of the American Art Collection. All rights reserved by Art Institute of Chicago © Estate of Grant Wood/DACS, London/VAGA, New York 2007 9bl; *Ritual Cache Figure* North American, New Mexico, Mimbres, Salado Region 10tl; *Tennessee, Entrance Hall*, 1835, 'Thorne Miniature Room' 10tc; *Panorama of Eight Views of*

Kanazawa under the Full Moon (1857) Ando Hiroshige, Clarence Buckingham Collection 10tr; *Triptych window from Avery Coonley Playhouse, Riverside, Illinois*, 1912 Frank Lloyd-Wright. © ARS, NY and DACS, London 2007 11tr; *Lampwork Paperweight: Clematis* c. 1848–55 Saint-Louis Factory, France 11cb; BUENA VISTA: 60bl; CHICAGO OFFICE OF TOURISM: 85bl; Mark Montgomery 106tc; Willie Schmidt 112c; Peter J. Schulz 50tl, 92tr; COLUMBIA PICTURES: 60tr; CORBIS: Alan Schein Photography 12–13c; Bettmann 35tl; Thomas A. Heinz 30clb; Jon Hicks1c; Sandy Felsenthal 30cla; COURT THEATRE: Mary Stuart by Friedrich Schiller. Translated by Robert David MacDonald. Directed by Joanne Akalaitis. Left to Right: Jenny Bacon and Barbara E. Robertson 48cla; DUSABLE MUSEUM: 99tr; THE FIELD MUSEUM: 6c, 14cla, 14c, 14br, 15tl, 15clb, 93c; FUNKY BUDDHA LOUNGE: 44tl; GENE SISKEL FILM CENTER: 48tr; GOLD COAST GUEST HOUSE: 114tl, 117tl; Courtesy of HERSHEY'S CHICAGO: 81br; INTERNATIONAL MUSEUM OF SURGICAL SCIENCES: 39tl; JOHN HANDLEY: 50bl, 64tl, 106tr, 108tr; JAMES LEMASS: 31clb, 106–107; JOHN G. SHEDD AQUARIUM 22cb, 22bl, 22–23c, 23tr, 23cr, 23bl, 56c; Edward G. Lines, Jnr 92c; LEONARDO MEDIA LIMITED: 115tl, 116tl, 116tr; LINCOLN PARK ZOO: 7tl, 24cla, 24bc, 24-25c, 25cr, 25clb; Todd Rosenberg 56tr; MARY EVANS PICTURE LIBRARY: 34t, 35d; MAYOR'S OFFICE OF SPECIAL EVENTS: 3tr, 50tc, 50tr, 51tl; MEXICAN MUSEUM OF FINE ART: Work by Jesus Helguera Courtesy of Garrison and Rosslyn Valentine 38bl; MUSEUM OF CONTEMPORARY ART: *Memorial to the Idea of Man If He Was an Idea* H.C. Westermann © DACS, London/VAGA, New York 2007 79c; MUSEUM OF SCIENCE & INDUSTRY: 16bl, 16bcl, 17tr,18tc, 18tr, 18c, 19c, 56tl; Scott Brownell 17cb; Dirk Fletcher 98cr; NATIONAL VIETNAM VETERANS MUSEUM: 95tl; *Goodbye Vietnam* David A. Sessions 38tl; NAVY PIER: 3bl, 6bl, 20cla, 20cb, 20–21c, 21tr, 21bl, 57tr; OLD TOWN SCHOOL OF FOLK MUSIC: 49tr; PARAMOUNT PICTURES: 60tl; PEGGY NOTEBAERT NATURE MUSEUM: 84tr; POSTER PLUS: 74tr; RESTAURANTS AMERICA: 96tr; RUSSIAN TEA-TIME: 75tl; SOFITEL CHICAGO WATER TOWER: 45tl; SOUTH SHORE CULTURAL CENTER: Brook Collins/Chicago Rark District 98tl; STEPPENWOLF THEATRE: 48tl; TERRA FOUNDATION OF THE ARTS: 81tl; UNIVERSITY OF CHICAGO: 7b, 29tl, 29cla, 29clb, 98tc; WATER TOWER PALACE: 107tr; WHEELER MANSION: 117tr.

All other images are © Dorling Kindersley. For further information see *www.dkimages.com*

Dorling Kindersley Special Editions

Dorling Kindersley books can be purchased in bulk quantities at discounted prices and we are able to offer editions tailored specifically to meet your own needs. To find out more, please contact (in the United Kingdom) - Sarah.Burgess@dk.com or Special Sales, Dorling Kindersley Limited, 80 Strand, London WC2R 0RL; (in the United States) – Special Markets Department, DK Publishing, Inc., 375 Hudson Street, New York, New York 10014.

Selected Street Index

Chicago's Grid System

Nearly all streets in Chicago run east–west or north–south. The zero point is at the intersection of Madison Street (running east-west) and State Street (running north-south). All streets are labelled in relation to this point: for example, the section of State Street north of Madison is known as North State Street. Numbering also begins at the zero point and odd numbers are on the east sides of north-south streets and the south sides of east-west streets.